The Black Death

By Don Nardo

LUCENT BOOKS

A part of Gale, Cengage Learning

GALE
CENGAGE Learning

Detroit • New York • San Francisco • New Haven, Conn • Waterville, Maine • London

GALE
CENGAGE Learning

LIBRARY OF CONGRESS CATALOGING-IN-PUBLICATION DATA

Nardo, Don, 1947–
    The Black Death / by Don Nardo.
        p. cm. -- (World history)
    Includes bibliographical references and index.
    ISBN 978-1-4205-0348-7
    1. Black Death--Juvenile literature. I. Title.
    RC172.N37 2011
    614.5'732--dc22

                                                2010043804

Lucent Books
27500 Drake Rd.
Farmington Hills, MI 48331

ISBN-13: 978-1-4205-0348-7
ISBN-10: 1-4205-0348-0

Printed in the United States of America
1 2 3 4 5 6 7 14 13 12 11 10

Printed by Bang Printing, Brainerd, MN, 1st Ptg., 02/2011

Contents

Foreword

Each year, on the first day of school, nearly every history teacher faces the task of explaining why his or her students should study history. Many reasons have been given. One is that lessons exist in the past from which contemporary society can benefit and learn. Another is that exploration of the past allows us to see the origins of our customs, ideas, and institutions. Concepts such as democracy, ethnic conflict, or even things as trivial as fashion or mores, have historical roots.

Reasons such as these impress few students, however. If anything, these explanations seem remote and dull to young minds. Yet history is anything but dull. And therein lies what is perhaps the most compelling reason for studying history: History is filled with great stories. The classic themes of literature and drama—love and sacrifice, hatred and revenge, injustice and betrayal, adversity and overcoming adversity—fill the pages of history books, feeding the imagination as well as any of the great works of fiction do.

The story of the Children's Crusade, for example, is one of the most tragic in history. In 1212 Crusader fever hit Europe. A call went out to the pope that all good Christians should journey to Jerusalem to drive out the hated Muslims and return the city to Christian control. Heeding the call, thousands of children made the journey. Parents bravely allowed many children to go, and entire communities were inspired by the faith of these small Crusaders. Unfortunately, many boarded ships captained by slave traders, who sold the children into slavery as soon as they arrived at their destination. Thousands died from disease, exposure, and starvation on the long march across Europe to the Mediterranean Sea. Others perished at sea.

Another story, from a modern and more familiar place, offers a soul-wrenching view of personal humiliation but also the ability to rise above it. Hatsuye Egami was one of 110,000 Japanese Americans sent to internment camps during World War II. "Since yesterday we Japanese have ceased to be human beings," he wrote in his diary. "We are numbers. We are no longer Egamis, but the number 23324. A tag with that number is on every trunk, suitcase and bag. Tags, also, on our breasts." Despite such dehumanizing treatment, most internees worked hard to control their bitterness. They created workable communities inside the camps and demonstrated again and again their loyalty as Americans.

These are but two of the many stories from history that can be found in the pages of the Lucent Books World History series. All World History titles rely on sound research and verifiable evidence, and all give students a clear sense of time, place, and chronology through maps and time lines as well as text.

All titles include a wide range of authoritative perspectives that demonstrate the complexity of historical interpretation and sharpen the reader's critical thinking skills. Formally documented quotations and annotated bibliographies enable students to locate and evaluate sources, often instantaneously via the Internet, and serve as valuable tools for further research and debate.

Finally, Lucent's World History titles present rousing good stories, featuring vivid primary source quotations drawn from unique, sometimes obscure sources such as diaries, public records, and contemporary chronicles. In this way, the voices of participants and witnesses as well as important biographers and historians bring the study of history to life. As we are caught up in the lives of others, we are reminded that we too are characters in the ongoing human saga, and we are better prepared for our own roles.

1349
The Black Death reaches the Netherlands, Scotland, Ireland, and Scandinavia.

1313
Giovanni Boccaccio, the Italian writer who will later write a famous description of the Black Death, is born.

1347
The Black Death arrives in Constantinople, Egypt, Sicily, and Italy.

1367
Pope Urban V moves the papacy's residence from Avignon, France, back to its traditional home in Rome

1361
A new outbreak of bubonic plague strikes parts of Europe.

1337
The Hundred Years War, fought between England and France, begins.

1310	1320	1330	1340	1350	1360	1370

1345–1346
The Mongols lay siege to Kaffa, a town on the Crimean peninsula; the attackers catapult plague-infected bodies into the town.

1350
An English war fleet commanded by King Edward III defeats a Spanish fleet near Winchelsea, on the southern English coast.

Edward III

1431
As the Hundred Years War rages on, French maid and war leader Joan of Arc is burned at the stake on charges of heresy.

1894
As an outbreak of the bubonic plague occurs in China, Swiss scientist Alexandre Yersin identifies the germ that causes the disease.

1385
Portugal achieves independence from Spain.

90	1405–1406	1431	1664	1776	1894	1900–1904

1405–1406
England suffers from the first major outbreak of plague in the fifteenth century.

1664
An unexpected outbreak of the plague kills some 70,000 people in London.

1900–1904
Bubonic plague strikes the U.S. city of San Francisco, where it kills 121 people.

1776
England's thirteen American colonies declare their independence, creating the United States.

The Wild Cards of History

"What I have to say is so extraordinary," Italian writer Giovanni Boccaccio wrote in 1350, "that if it had not been so often witnessed, and I had not seen it with my own eyes, I could scarcely believe it, let alone write about it." Agonizing fear had become so powerful and widespread, Boccaccio said, that

> brothers abandoned each other, uncles abandoned their nephews, sisters abandoned their brothers, and wives frequently abandoned their husbands. And there is something else that is almost incredible. Fathers and mothers were loathe to visit and care for their children, almost as if they did not belong to them.[1]

This harrowing account, which appears near the start of Boccaccio's famous work, the *Decameron*, is not fictional. Rather, Boccaccio is describing the onset of one of the worst natural disasters in recorded history. Just two years before he took up his pen to write these words, a horrifying disease epidemic struck his hometown of Florence, Italy. At the same time, the disease was beginning to ravage Greece, Spain, France, and other parts of southern Europe. People also started contracting it in Palestine, Egypt, and across North Africa. In the short span of about four years, the disease killed at least 25 million people in Europe alone. Many millions more succumbed in the regions bordering Europe. The disease not only killed people with abandon, but it also wiped out the populations of entire towns, destroyed national economies, altered numerous political and social institutions, and changed the way many people felt about God and the church. Most scholars agree, says historian Robert S. Gottfried,

> that it was not until the mid–sixteenth century that Europe regained its

thirteenth-century population levels. And in the late fourteenth and fifteenth centuries, dominated by depopulation and manpower shortages, came changes which profoundly influenced the course of Western history.[2]

At the time, the Europeans and others who suffered from this biological onslaught had no idea what was killing them. They called it the "Great Pestilence" or "Great Plague." (It did not acquire the name "Black Death" until several centuries later.) They did not realize that the culprit was a microbe, or germ, associated with a highly contagious disease called bubonic plague. In fact, they, including their finest doctors, did not even know what microbes were. Unfortunately for them, the discovery of the germ theory of disease was still five centuries in the future. All they knew for sure was that it was the worst catastrophe of any kind in living memory.

Biblical Plagues

For centuries before the Black Death, no large-scale outbreaks of serious illness had spread through Europe and nearby

Recording the Symptoms

As described by Byzantine historian Procopius, the symptoms of the disease that struck Constantinople (present-day Istanbul, Turkey) in A.D. 541 indicate what modern science has determined to be the bubonic plague. Procopius wrote:

With the majority [of victims] it came about that they were seized by the disease without becoming aware of what was coming either through a waking vision or a dream. And they were taken in the following manner. They had a sudden fever.... And the body showed no change from its previous color, nor was it hot as might be expected when attacked by a fever.... It was natural, therefore, that not one of those who had contracted the disease expected to die from it. But on the same day in some cases, in others on the following day, and in the rest not many days later, a bubonic swelling developed; and this took place not only in the particular part of the body which is ... below the abdomen, but also inside the arm-pit, and in some cases also beside the ears, and at different points on the thighs.

Procopius, *History of the Wars*, trans. H.B. Dewing. Cambridge, MA: Harvard University Press, 1935, pp. 457–58.

The Bible's Old Testament records instances of plague. People said that they were divine punishments.

regions. However, the profound and terrifying event was by no means the first time that a disease epidemic had affected the fates of nations and peoples. Indeed, numerous written accounts of such dire events have survived from past ages.

Among the oldest of these writings are several that appear in the biblical Old Testament. As was true of Europeans and others in the 1300s, people in biblical times did not know about germs and their role in causing disease. This is partly why the numerous disease epidemics mentioned in the Bible were then thought to be divine punishments for various human transgressions. One of the more famous episodes of this type is found in the book of Exodus. It tells how God struck down the firstborn sons of Egypt to persuade that nation's king to allow the enslaved Hebrews to leave. Some scholars point out that the episode might be a distant and somewhat distorted memory of a disease epidemic.

Another large-scale disease outbreak appears in the book of Isaiah. It describes what happened when the Assyrian king Sennacherib laid siege to Jerusalem, capital of the Jewish kingdom of Judah, in 701 B.C. According to Isaiah:

> thus says the Lord concerning the king of Assyria: He shall not come into this city or shoot an arrow there or come before it with a shield or cast up a siege mound against it … for I will defend this city to save it…. And the angel of the Lord went out and struck down a hundred and eighty-five thousand in the camp of

the Assyrians. And when [the Jews] arose early in the morning, behold, these were all dead bodies.[3]

Some historians insist that this story was made up later. They suggest that the Assyrians left Judah after its ruler, Hezekiah, paid Sennacherib off with large amounts of gold and silver. Still, the possibility of disease playing a role remains. Noted American historian William H. McNeill proposed that during the siege a number of Assyrian soldiers might have contracted cholera and/or other waterborne illnesses. Eventually, according to this view, their king decided that capturing the city was not worth the effort. In addition McNeill suggests that the number of deaths seems unrealistic. "The figure of 185,000 disease deaths must be vastly exaggerated," he writes. "No ancient army came close to such a size, much less one operating in the barren environs of Jerusalem."[4]

Europe Periodically Ravaged

If nothing else, biblical speculations about disease outbreaks are reminders that such events can and often have had major historical consequences. In the words of American military historian Robert Cowley, "Disease has to be counted as one of the wild cards of history, an unforeseen factor that can, in a matter of days or weeks, undo the [most determined plans and efforts] or humble the conquering momentum."[5]

A famous example from ancient times of disease humbling a major military power is the plague that struck the Greek city-state of Athens in 430 B.C. At the time it was one of the two superpowers among the Greek states (each of which viewed itself as a separate nation). The other was Sparta. The Spartans and their allies went to war in 431, and when the Spartans attacked Athenian territory the following year, the Athenians took refuge behind their secure city walls. Then, quite unexpectedly, and with frightening swiftness, the epidemic struck. The Athenian historian Thucydides, who later penned a chronicle of the war, described it in these words:

> People in perfect health suddenly began to have burning feelings in the head. Their eyes became red and inflamed. Inside their mouths there was bleeding from the throat and tongue, and the breath became unnatural and unpleasant…. Before long, the pain settled on the chest and was accompanied by coughing. Next the stomach was affected, with stomach-aches and with vomiting…. The skin was rather reddish and livid, breaking out into small pustules [boils] and ulcers…. If people survived this critical period, then the disease descended into the bowels, producing violent … and uncontrollable diarrhea, so that most of them died later as a result of the weakness caused by this. It affected the genitals, fingers, and toes, and many of those who recovered lost the use of these members. Some, too, went blind.[6]

The malady Thucydides described remains unidentified. What is more certain is that it killed at least 20 percent of Athens's residents, including its leading general and statesman, Pericles. Several factors contributed to the city's ultimate defeat in the war, but the loss of the tremendously talented Pericles and so many of his countrymen to disease was certainly one of the major ones.

The Greeks were not the only early Europeans who were periodically ravaged by epidemics of unknown origins. The Romans, whose empire was Europe's largest and most powerful in ancient times, endured the onset of three enormous and deadly epidemics in the span of fewer than four centuries. The first was probably caused by smallpox. It struck Italy and other parts of the western Roman realm between A.D. 165 and 180. The greatest physician of the age, Galen, estimated that at least a quarter of Italy's population died. The second great disease outbreak—likely measles—struck between 251 and 260, killing up to five thousand people a day in the city of Rome alone.

The third and most destructive epidemic to decimate the Roman world appeared in 541. It eventually became known as "Justinian's Plague," after the emperor who ruled the eastern Roman sphere (later called the Byzantine Empire), which was devastated by it. According to the Byzantine historian Procopius:

> During these times there was a pestilence, by which the whole human race came near to being annihilated.

Now in the case of all other scourges [blights] sent from Heaven some explanation of a cause might be given by daring men, such as the many theories propounded by those who are clever in these matters.... But for this calamity it is quite impossible either to express in words or to conceive in thought any explanation, except indeed to refer it to [cite the cause as] God.[7]

God's "Quivering Spear"

Justinian's Plague was particularly notable for three reasons. First, it was startlingly widespread in extent. Its effects were felt as far west as Ireland and as far east as southern Asia. Second, it was horribly lethal. Approximately 40 percent of the citizens of the imperial capital, Constantinople (present-day Istanbul, Turkey), died, as did an estimated one-fourth of the population of southern Europe.

The third reason the epidemic was significant was that the disease it unleashed was bubonic plague. Thus, the outbreak of the 500s gave Europe its first nasty taste of a microbial murderer that would exterminate even more Europeans in the great outbreak of the 1300s. Because eight centuries separated the two events,

those who suffered in the later one had no memory of the earlier one. For that reason, the second colossal assault of the Black Death to strike Europe seemed to have no precedent. Most people viewed it as so huge and unique that only God could be responsible for it. That explanation—divine wrath—became a major theme of the age, a warning that would echo down the corridors of history until the rise of medical science, which would offer an alternative explanation. In 1348, at the height of the horror, Italian lawyer Gabriel de Mussis wrote:

May this stand as a perpetual reminder to everyone, now living and yet to be born, how almighty God ... lord of the living and of the dead, [peered] down from heaven and saw the entire human race wallowing in the mire of manifold [diverse kinds of] wickedness. [After the Lord warned people to stop sinning and they refused], disease was sent forth. The quivering spear of the Almighty was aimed everywhere and infected the whole human race with its pitiless wounds.... Mourn, mourn you peoples, and call upon the mercy of God.[8]

Chapter One

Onset of the Black Death

Looking back, it is fairly easy to see why the Black Death killed so many Europeans in the fourteenth century. Two often-cited reasons are that no one knew what caused it and that there was no cure. Of equal importance, however, was the fact that people were not at all prepared for such an enormous and terrifying onslaught of disease.

In large part this lack of preparedness was the result of Europe's having been unusually free of large disease epidemics for several centuries before the Black Death. With a few isolated exceptions, most of the ailments that affected local populations in the early medieval era were associated with malnutrition or famine. Malnutrition, for example, occurs when the body fails to get enough nutrition, and it can cause vitamin deficiencies, anemia (a serious shortage of the body's red blood cells), skin conditions, and severe diarrhea. There were also periodic outbreaks of ergotism (then

called Saint Anthony's fire), a kind of poisoning caused by a fungus that infects rye and other grains. Leprosy (also called Hansen's disease), a chronic infection that can badly disfigure the face and limbs, was also an ever-present problem. However, it is not very contagious. Also, leprosy is only occasionally fatal.

Indeed, all of these illnesses were, variously, not contagious, mildly contagious, and/or mostly confined to individual neighborhoods, cities, or regions. None were nearly as heinous and lethal as the Black Death, which was extremely contagious and spread rapidly from town to town and country to country.

Still another reason that the human toll from the Black Death was so high was that Europe had a large number of potential victims. During the relatively disease-free period from the 600s to the early 1300s, the continent's population increased significantly. It grew by 300 percent between the 900s and late

The Black Death in the fourteenth century brought death to Europe on a never before seen scale. Families abandoned one another in a quest to save themselves.

1200s alone. As a result, by the mid-1300s Europe had at least 75 million people.

These multitudes were unprepared for the onset of sickness and death on a massive scale and had no conception of the other destructive effects such an epidemic can cause. When the epidemic began to spread, this ignorance escalated into fear. Dread of both death and the unknown was so consuming and overwhelming that it often caused the structure of civilized life and society to break down. Incidents such as those Boccaccio had observed of parents abandoning their children and brothers deserting

brothers were repeated countless times across the continent. It is no wonder that even those who lived through the calamity thought their entire world was coming to an end.

Origins in Central Asia

Although fourteenth-century Europeans did not know what caused the Black Death and were unprepared for it, they did have a credible idea of where it came from. Several writers of that time, including the Italian Gabriel de Mussis, claimed it entered Europe from the "East." To Europeans, the East was (and often still is)

Evidence near Lake Balkhash, in present day Kazakhstan, indicates that the Black Death originated far east of Europe.

a general term for Asia, including the region now called the Middle East.

Modern experts confirm this assumption. They found convincing evidence that the germs that caused the great epidemic originated far to the east of Europe. One of the key clues was the discovery, in 1885, of an old graveyard near the ruins of a medieval Christian community not far south of Lake Balkhash. (That extensive waterway lies in south-central Asia, due north of India.) In the cemetery a Russian archaeologist found an abnormally large number of graves that were dug in 1338 and 1339. Moreover, three of the headstones named as the cause of death the disease later identified as bubonic plague.

Scientists believe that the malady reached the Lake Balkhash area from somewhere in central Asia. Almost certainly it first spread from animals to humans in that region. According to distinguished medical researcher Alfred J. Bollet:

In this area of central Asia, marmots [large ground squirrels] were trapped for their fur, which was then sold to various traders who shipped them along [local] caravan routes. Hunters and trappers were always happy to find sick or dying animals that they could catch easily, and around this time many untrapped marmots were found dead. Trappers skinned these animals and sent the furs to be shipped to buyers in the West. Bales of marmot fur probably contained living fleas [infected with plague] that became very hungry without a live animal on which to feed…. The furs reached [towns along the trade routes] and, when the bales were opened, the hungry fleas jumped out [and onto humans].[9]

From central Asia, the disease moved southward into India. It also made its way westward along the major trade routes leading to the Black Sea area. At the time, much of western Asia was dominated by the Mongols (whom many in the West called Tartars). By the mid-1340s many Mongols and others in the region had died of the plague, which next struck the Crimea. (The highly populated Crimean Peninsula juts out into the Black Sea's northern reaches.)

There, in the winter of 1345–1346, a Mongol war leader was attempting to capture the town of Kaffa, a thriving colony of the Genoese, whose home city

This map shows the supposed path of the plague in the fourteenth century.

of Genoa, in northwestern Italy, was one of Europe's great trading centers. Soon the Mongols had more to deal with than the besieged Genoese. According to Mussis, "the whole army was affected by a disease which overran the Tartars and killed thousands upon thousands every day." He added that "all medical advice and attention was useless. The Tartars died as soon as the signs of disease appeared on their bodies."[10] Seeing what the unknown ailment was doing to his own soldiers, the Mongol chieftain decided to employ what today is referred to as biological warfare. As noted British scholar Philip Ziegler tells it:

> they used their giant catapults to lob over the walls [of Kaffa] the corpses of the [Mongol] victims in the hope that this would spread the disease within the city. As fast as the rotting bodies arrived in their midst, the Genoese carried them through the town and dropped them into the sea. But few places are so vulnerable to disease as a besieged city and it was not long before the plague was as active within the city as without.[11]

The Pestilence Invades Europe

With so many people dying inside Kaffa, those who were still living naturally felt desperate to escape. A fair number of Genoese did manage to board ships and sail southward into the Black Sea, not realizing they were carrying with them swarms

An Italian artist depicts the plague's indiscriminate assault on the people of Italy in the fourteenth century. Cities along the seacoast were the first to experience the plague.

of tiny, invisible, and lethal killers. They brought these microscopic assassins first to Constantinople [present-day Istanbul, Turkey], the mighty Byzantine metropolis on the sea's southern shore. From the dock areas, the contagion speedily spread into the city's streets. No neighborhood or building—small or large, rich or poor—was immune, and by mid-1347 the inhabitants were dying by the thousands.

But much worse was to come, for Constantinople was a busy hub for traders from across the Mediterranean-European sphere. Ships inadvertently carrying the disease now headed southward into the Mediterranean, bound for ports in Palestine, Egypt, North Africa, Greece, Italy, and beyond. Not long afterward, a Byzantine observer wrote, "A plague attacked almost all the seacoasts of the world and killed most of the people."[12]

Italy was one of first regions to feel the deadly impact. About sixteen vessels carried the plague there late in 1347, three to Genoa, one to Venice, and twelve to Messina, in Sicily. Italian writer Michael of Piazza described the initial and crucial outbreak in Messina:

At the beginning of October ... twelve Genoese galleys [arrived in] the harbor of Messina. In their bones they bore so virulent [potent] a disease that anyone who only spoke to them was seized by a mortal illness and in no manner could evade death. The infection spread to everyone who had any contact with the diseased [people]. Not only all those who had speech with them died, but also those who had touched or used any of their things. When the inhabitants of Messina discovered that this sudden death emanated from the Genoese ships, they hurriedly ordered them out of the harbor and town. But the evil remained and caused a fearful outbreak of death.[13]

Messina Ravaged by the Plague

Italian writer Michael of Piazza described the terrifying spread of the plague through the Italian city of Messina in 1348:

Soon men hated each other so much that if a son was attacked by the disease his father would not tend him. If, in spite of all, he dared to approach him, he was immediately infected and was bound to die within three days. Nor was this all; all those dwelling in the same house with him, even the cats and other domestic animals, followed him in death. As the number of deaths increased in Messina many desired to confess their sins to the priests and to draw up their last will and testament. But ecclesiastics [churchmen], lawyers and notaries refused to enter the houses of the diseased. Soon the corpses were lying forsaken in the houses. No ecclesiastic, no son, no father and no relation dared to enter, but they hired servants with high wages to bury the dead.

Quoted in Johannes Nohl, *The Black Death*, trans. C.H. Clarke. London: Allen and Unwin, 1926, p. 19.

From Europe's ports, the Black Death next raged inland, moving northward and eastward. In Italy it struck all the urban areas (cities and large towns) with a fury, including Padua, Pisa, Rome, and Florence. Michael of Piazza describes some of the frightening symptoms:

> Those infected felt themselves penetrated by a pain throughout their whole bodies and, so to say, undermined. Then there developed on the thighs or upper arms a boil about the size of a lentil which the people called "burn boil." This infected the whole body, and penetrated it so that the patient violently vomited blood. This vomiting of blood continued without intermission for three days, there being no means of healing it, and then the patient expired [died].[14]

"The City was Full of Corpses"

So many people succumbed in each town that the streets became littered with corpses. Among the more vivid surviving descriptions is that of Italian writer Giovanni Boccaccio, who witnessed the devastation in his native Florence. Many people "finished up [their lives] on the streets," he said, "and those who did die in their homes only made their neighbors aware of their death by the stench from their corrupted [decomposing] bodies." Indeed, he continued:

> The city was full of corpses. Most of them were dealt with in the same way by their neighbors, influenced as much by fear of being infected by the rotting bodies as by charity towards the dead. By themselves, or with the aid of bearers … they dragged the newly dead out of their homes and placed them on their doorsteps, where anyone who passed by, particularly in the morning, could see countless numbers of them…. Things [became so terrible] that dead human beings were treated no better than goats.[15]

The problem of large numbers of dead bodies lying in the open in Florence, as well as in other cities, was compounded by another dilemma. Namely, no one wanted to touch these corpses. This was only natural, since people feared they might contract the contagion through bodily contact (although they had no idea how such contact might transmit it). As a result, very few were willing to take on the appalling task of burying the dead. In most cases, people ended up paying low-class thugs and criminals to do it. According to Boccaccio,

> few bodies were accompanied to church by more than ten or a dozen of their neighbors, and even these were not respected citizens. Instead, a band of scavengers, drawn from the dregs of society bore the bier [coffin]. (They call themselves gravediggers, and they gave their services at a price.) And they bore it in a hurry, usually not to the church which had been chosen but simply

to the nearest [church]. [They and a few priests] put the body as quickly as they could into any unoccupied grave.[16]

Still another problem associated with the masses of dead, contaminated bodies was where to bury them. Most Europeans were Christians and expected that when they passed on they would be laid in sacred ground, usually cemeteries adjoining churches. But as Boccaccio pointed out,

There was not enough consecrated [sacred] ground to bury the great multitude of corpses arriving at every church every day and almost every hour. [So] when all the graves were occupied, very deep pits were dug in the churchyards, into which the new arrivals were put in [the] hundreds. As they were stowed there, one on top of another, like merchandise in the hold of a ship, each layer was covered with a little earth, until the pit was full.[17]

Fear of death and the instinct for self-preservation overcame the population, Boccaccio sadly observed. Feeling compelled to comment on the breakdown of morals and civil behavior he saw occurring around him, he wrote:

I have frequently [seen people during the plague outbreak] who make

"A Rootless Phantom"

In the year after the Black Death struck the British Isles, a Welsh poet named Jeuan Gethin penned this lament, which emphasizes the unsightly, painful lumps the disease caused on people's bodies.

We see death coming into our midst like black smoke, a plague which cuts off the young, a rootless phantom which has no mercy or fair countenance [good looks]. Woe is me of the shilling [lump] in the arm-pit; it is seething, terrible, wherever it may come, a head that gives pain and causes a loud cry, a burden carried under the arms, a painful angry knob, a white lump. It is of the form of an apple, like the head of an onion, a small boil that spares no-one. Great is its seething, like a burning cinder, a grievous thing of an ashy color. It is an ugly eruption that comes with unseemly haste. It is a grievous ornament that breaks out in a rash. The early ornaments [signs of impending] of black death.

Quoted in Mike Ibeji, "Black Death," BBC, www.bbc.co.uk/history/british/middle_ages/black_01.shtml.

no distinction between right and wrong, but only consider their appetites, and simply do … whatever gives them most pleasure. I am speaking not only of lay-people [nonclergy], but of monks in their monasteries who, having … broken their rule of obedience, [have] given themselves over to carnal [sexual] delights and become lascivious [lustful] and dissolute [depraved], hoping by this means to avoid the plague. If this is true, and it obviously is, what are we doing here? [What] are we thinking of? [Do] we believe that our lives are bound to our bodies by stronger ties than other people's are, and consequently imagine that we need not bother about anything with power to harm them? [How] foolish we are to think like this![18]

Forming a Deadly Noose

Other distressed observers witnessed similar signs of selfishness and indifference (amid occasional acts of kindness) inspired by the colossal epidemic as it spread northward into the heart of Europe. One was French chronicler Jean de Venette. Describing the plague's swift and shocking passage through his native land, he wrote:

Pope Clement VI resided at the Palace of the Popes in Avignon, France, shown here. Avignon was also struck by the plague, which killed half the town in only a few weeks.

Nothing like the great numbers who died in the years 1348 and 1349 has been heard of or seen in times past.... If a well man visited the sick he only rarely evaded the risk of death. [As a result] in many towns timid priests withdrew, leaving the exercise of their ministry to such of the religious as were more daring. In many places not two out of twenty remained alive. So high was the mortality [death toll] at the Hôtel-Dieu [hospital] in Paris that for a long time, more than five hundred dead were carried daily with great devotion in carts to the cemetery of the Holy Innocents in Paris for burial. A very great number of the saintly sisters [nuns] of the Hôtel-Dieu who, not fearing to die, [courageously] nursed the sick in all sweetness and humility, with no thought of honor [or their own safety].[19]

The epidemic also struck Avignon, the French city where Pope Clement VI lived and held court on behalf of Europe's tens of millions of Christians. (The Roman Catholic Church, normally based in Rome, made Avignon its official headquarters from 1309 to 1378.) A leading member of that religious court reported, to his horror, that half the town's residents died in the outbreak's first two weeks alone. He further observed:

Within the walls of the city, there are now more than seven thousand houses shut up. In those no one is living, and all who have inhabited them are departed. The suburbs hardly contain any people at all. A field near [the church] "Our Lady of Miracles" has been bought by the Pope and consecrated as a cemetery. In this, from the 13th of March [1348], eleven thousand corpses have been buried. This does not include those interred [buried] in the cemetery of the hospital of St. Anthony, in cemeteries belonging to the religious bodies, and in many others which exist in Avignon.[20]

After nearly all of France had been engulfed by the wave of infection, the disease reached the shores of the English Channel. The English had fervently hoped that the wide waterway would protect them from the oncoming natural catastrophe. But this proved to be wishful thinking. Carried by rats that stowed away on boats, the Black Death leapt across the channel late in 1348. It proceeded to carve a path of misery, fear, and larger-scale fatality from southern England northward. Less than a year later, it reached the Scottish highlands and eastern Ireland.

Meanwhile, unsuspecting traders and travelers spread the plague through what are now Germany, Poland, and Russia. The Russian city of Moscow was devastated in 1352. There, the leader of the Russian Orthodox Church, along with tens of thousands of his flock, were dying in agony at the same time that the epidemic was heading southward toward another Russian city, Kiev.

When that crowded city, too, became a cauldron of mass death, no one there or anywhere else was aware of a strange, ironic twist of fate. Modern scholars have determined that the killer contagion reached Kiev by an unusually roundabout route. Instead of moving directly northward to Kiev from the Crimea in 1347, it made its way southward into the Mediterranean, decimated southern Europe, assaulted northern Europe, and from there, nearly five years later, entered Russia and attacked Kiev. "Launched at Kaffa in the Crimea, and now attaining Kiev some 700 kilometers [435 miles] to the north," historian David Herlihy remarks, "the plague almost closed a deadly noose around Europe."[21]

Something Unparalleled and Unnatural

The great catastrophe forming that immense noose affected animals as well as people. With few or no humans left to attend to them in many areas, domestic livestock—including sheep, pigs, goats, chickens, and even oxen—ran wild. Many of these beasts died from plague in the same manner that people did. English chronicler and befuddled eyewitness Henry Knighton reported:

There was a great murrain [mass death] of sheep everywhere in the kingdom, so that in one place in a single pasture more than 5,000 sheep died; and they putrefied [rotted] so that neither bird nor beast would touch them…. Sheep and cattle ran at large through the fields and among the crops, and there was none to drive them off or herd them; for lack of care they perished in ditches and hedges in incalculable numbers throughout all districts, and none knew what to do.[22]

Large numbers of wild creatures also died from the disease. At the same time, other animals seemed to sense that people were in disarray and helpless and boldly moved into human areas. One troubled observer describes the threatening antics of wolves and other creatures normally confined to the German woodlands:

Savage wolves roamed about in packs at night and howled round the walls of the towns. In the villages they did not slake their thirst for human blood by lurking in secret places … but boldly entered open houses and tore children from their mothers' sides. Indeed, they not only attacked children, but armed men, and overcame them…. They seemed no longer wild animals, but demons. Other creatures forsook [left behind] their woods. [For example] ravens in innumerable flocks flew over the towns with loud croaking. The kite [a bird of prey] and the vulture were heard in the air, [and] on houses the cuckoos and owls alighted and filled the night with their mournful lament.[23]

All of these weird, calamitous, and frightening events combined to convey

Domestic livestock, such as pigs and sheep, ran wild without farmers, who had been killed by the plague, to tend to them. These animals also became victims of the Black Death.

an impression that something unparalleled, unnatural, and horribly momentous was occurring. Moreover, it was clearly not happening on a random, haphazard basis. Rather, it seemed to be taking place everywhere and affecting all aspects of nature and human society. A native of Siena, Italy, who lost all five of his children to the Black Death, aptly summed up what so many other Europeans thought about the extraordinarily horrific disaster. "No bells tolled [for the dead]," he wrote. "And nobody wept no matter what his loss because almost everyone expected death." He added, "People said and [sincerely] believed, 'This is the end of the world.'"[24]

Chapter Two

Gripped by Fear
and Hysteria

Reactions by Europeans to the deadly onset of the great pestilence in the mid-1300s were, not surprisingly, diverse and intense. In some cases they were irrational, hysterical, or even violent. Some people searched for omens to determine if they had been warned of the disaster in advance and had ignored said warnings. (Omens are supposedly supernatural signs of major events, either good or bad, to come.) Others desperately tried to explain what was causing the devastating epidemic in order to ward it off. These attempts invariably failed. Still others reacted with such fear and hysteria that they engaged in self-mutilation or persecuted and/or killed innocent people.

Many Misguided Theories

The idea that the births of noteworthy persons, natural disasters, and other major events are preceded by omens was very common in ancient and medieval times. It was to be expected, therefore, that the onslaught of the Black Death would motivate people to look for odd happenings that had preceded the epidemic. Some recalled that unusually heavy mists had blanketed several European regions in 1347. Others remembered seeing falling stars (which are nothing more than tiny meteors burning up in the atmosphere). Earthquakes were also singled out. One purported omen that many people called attention to was described by French monk and chronicler Jean de Venette:

In the month of August, 1348, after Vespers [evening worship] when the sun was beginning to set, a big and very bright star appeared above Paris, toward the west. It did not seem, as stars usually do, to be very high above our hemisphere but rather very near. As the sun set and night came on, this star did not seem

In medieval times, it was common to believe that omens preceded major events, including natural disasters. This tapestry scene shows a man warning the king of the omen brought by a comet (shown at upper left).

to me or to many other friars who were watching it to move from one place. At length, when night had come, this big star, to the amazement of all of us who were watching, broke into many different rays and, as it shed these rays over Paris toward the east, totally disappeared and was completely annihilated. Whether it was a comet or not, whether it was composed of airy exhalations and was finally resolved into vapor, I leave to the decision of astronomers. It is, however, possible that it was a presage [omen] of the amazing pestilence to come, which, in fact, followed very shortly in Paris and throughout France and elsewhere.[25]

Modern scholars think that Venette and the others witnessed a large meteor that broke into pieces as it plunged through the atmosphere. Other theories people proposed to explain the source and identity of the plague were as misguided as de Venette's meteor theory. For instance, there were reports, mostly undocumented, of great storms in various far-eastern lands. Some people suggested that these tempests had blown the pestilence to Europe. Another common culprit blamed for the outbreak was earthquakes. Supposedly these had unleashed foul vapors from deep within the earth, which, when inhaled by humans, made them sick.

Uncanny, unnatural movements of the planets were also cited. Somehow, a number of people frantically reasoned, these heavenly high jinks caused the air on Earth to become corrupt and thereby infect humans with terrible ailments. This "impure air" hypothesis had the backing of many learned scholars of the day, including noted physicians. In October 1348 a group of French doctors asserted:

[Illness] can be caused by the corruption of water or food … yet we still regard illnesses proceeding from the corruption of the air as much more dangerous. This is because bad air is more noxious than food or drink in that it can penetrate quickly to the heart and lungs to do its damage. We believe that the present epidemic or plague has arisen from air corrupt in its substance, and not changed in its attributes. By which we wish it [to] be understood that air, being pure and clear by nature, can only become putrid or corrupt by being mixed with something else, that is to say, with evil vapors.[26]

The Wrath of the Gods

Many other reasons were given for the spread of the plague. But none was more widespread and accepted than the idea that it was a punishment sent by God. In September 1348 an English priest ably summed up this view, stating:

Terrible is God toward the sons of men and by his command all things are subdued to the rule of his will. Those whom he loves he censures [condemns] and chastises [punishes]; that is, he punishes their shameful deeds in various ways during this mortal life so that they might not be condemned eternally. He often allows plagues, miserable famines, conflicts, wars and other forms of suffering to arise, and uses them to terrify and torment men and so drive out their sins. And thus, indeed, the realm of England, because of the growing pride and corruption of its subjects, and their numberless sins … is to be oppressed by the pestilence.[27]

God was not the only supernatural entity blamed for bringing on the plague. As the widely respected scholar of medieval times Barbara W. Tuchman tells it:

Scandinavians believed that a Pest Maiden emerged from the mouth of the dead in the form of a blue flame and flew through the air to infect the next house. In Lithuania, the Maiden was said to wave a red scarf through the door or window to let in the pest. One brave man, according to legend, deliberately waited at his open window with drawn sword and, at the fluttering of the scarf, chopped off the hand. He died of his deed, but his village was spared and the scarf [was] long preserved as a relic in the local church.[28]

Antiplague Ordinances

These passages, which seem so bizarre and naive today, demonstrate the sad fact that medieval doctors had no clue as to what caused the epidemic. They also did not know how to treat people for the symptoms of the disease. On the other hand, it did seem apparent to doctors, as well as many laymen, that the plague was somehow contagious. For this reason, a number of towns implemented travel restrictions, rules for public hygiene, and quarantines (separating plague victims from healthy persons).

One well-documented example is a decree containing antiplague ordinances issued in May 1348 in the Italian town of Pistoia. "No citizen of Pistoia," it said, "shall in any way dare or presume to go to Pisa or Lucca or to the county or district of either." Similarly, no one

The town of Pistoia, Italy, issued an anti-plague ordinance preventing its citizens from traveling to the neighboring towns of Pisa and Lucca, as well as travelers from those towns from entering Pistoia.

No Wailing Allowed

On the long list of plague ordinances decreed in Pistoia, Italy, were the following:

> They [wise men of the city] have provided and ordered that no paid mourner ... shall dare or presume to mourn publicly or privately or to invite other citizens of Pistoia to go to the funeral or to the dead person; nor may anyone engage [hire] the foresaid mourner, horn-player, cryer or drummer. So that the sounds of bells might not depress the infirm nor fear arise in them [the wise men] have provided and ordered that the bell-ringers or custodians in charge of the bell-tower of the cathedral of Pistoia shall not permit any bell [to] be rung for the funeral of the dead nor shall any person dare or presume to ring any of these bells on the said occasion.... They have provided and ordered that no person should dare or presume to raise or cause to be raised any wailing or clamor over any person or because of any person who has died outside the city, district or county of Pistoia ... on a penalty of 25 lira.

"Ordinances for Sanitation in a Time of Mortality," Institute for Advanced Technology in the Humanities, www2.iath.virginia.edu/osheim/pistoia.html.

was allowed to travel from those cities to Pistoia; if they did, they had to pay a penalty of 50 lira. Some of the other rules in the decree included:

> No person [shall] dare or presume in any way to bring [to Pistoia] any used cloth, either linen or woolen, for use as clothing for men or women or for bedclothes on penalty of 200 lira.... The bodies of the dead [cannot be] removed from the place in which they are found unless first such a body has been placed in a wooden casket covered by a lid secured with nails, so that no stench can issue forth from it.... In order to avoid the foul stench which the bodies of the dead give off ... any ditch in which a dead body is to be buried must be dug under ground to a depth of 2 1/2 braccia [arm lengths] by the measure of the city of Pistoia.... Butchers and retail vendors of meat [cannot] slaughter meat animals nor hang them after slaughter in any stable or other place in which there is any stench, on a penalty of 10 lira.[29]

Authorities in Venice issued similar rules in March 1348. Venetians who had died of the plague had to be buried at least 5 feet (1.5m) deep. Also, infected citizens were quarantined by being taken to uninhabited islands and no foreign vessels were allowed to dock in the city for forty days. (No one could predict how long the epidemic would last; forty days was chosen because it is the amount of time the Bible says that Jesus Christ suffered in the wilderness.)

Despite these earnest efforts, the plague killed a hundred thousand people, some 60 percent of Venice's residents, over the eighteen months that followed. Among the dead were many doctors. Of those physicians who lived, most fled the city, leaving their patients to suffer in agony. One exception was a doctor named Francesco, who remained at his post throughout the crisis. When asked why he did not run away like his fellow physicians had, he replied, "I would rather die here than live elsewhere."[30]

Similar attempts to stop the spread of the plague abounded across Europe. But these were also largely futile because no one realized that the disease was transmitted by fleas and rats. As a result, they did not keep these carriers of the sickness away from healthy people, with catastrophic consequences.

Common Scapegoats

Because nothing substantial was known about the causes of the Black Death, a number of frightened, desperate people searched for individuals and/or groups to blame. Almost always these scapegoats dwelled outside of society's mainstream and for one reason or another had long been perceived as odd or suspicious. A surgeon in the French city of Avignon described some of the more common scapegoats whom he witnessed being persecuted:

In some places … they drove out paupers [poor people] who were deformed. In others they drove out nobles. This finally [got so bad] that guards were posted to see that no one who was not well known would enter a city or village. And if they found anyone carrying medicinal powders [ground-up herbs], they would force them to swallow them to prove that they were not poisonous potions.[31]

Poor people and outsiders were not the only people targeted. Also suspected of bringing on the plague were mentally ill and physically challenged people who lived on society's fringes. According to scholar James C. Giblin:

On the edges of many villages, in poor huts made of sticks and straw, lived outcasts of various kinds. Some were deformed from birth, others were simple-minded, still others were insane. The villagers gave them names like Poor Tom and Mad Mag. The majority were harmless, although children sometimes taunted them and called the old women witches. Most adults

This image shows Death, left, with a Jewish man. Jews were blamed for the plague in Europe. They were used as scapegoats to explain what was happening, and were often tortured into "confessions" or killed.

simply left them alone. That changed when the Black Death came. As more people sickened and died, the survivors became increasingly frustrated. Neither the village priest nor the barber surgeon had a solution for the plague.... Maybe the children were right, [many villagers] thought. Maybe Mad Mag really was a witch. If they got rid of her, maybe the pestilence would finally go away.[32]

Another widespread speculation, one based not only on fear but also on extreme bigotry, was that Jews were responsible for the plague. Supposedly they had poisoned wells and other supplies of drinking water in order to exterminate Christians. "Some wretched men were found in possession of certain powders," reported an Italian commentator in April 1348.

> And, whether justly or unjustly, God knows, [they] were accused of poisoning the wells—with the result that anxious men now refuse to drink water from wells. Many were burned for this and are being burned daily, for it was ordered that they be punished thus.[33]

The Blood Libel

It is only natural to wonder why so many people believed Jews had caused the great epidemic. Part of the answer is that Jews had been unfairly blamed and persecuted for all manner of crimes for centuries. More specifically, much of the distrust and hatred for Jews stemmed from the so-called blood libel. Tuchman explains:

> Promoted by popular preachers, a mythology of blood grew in a mirror image of [Holy Communion], the Christian ritual of drinking [wine to symbolize] the blood of the Savior [Jesus]. Jews were believed to kidnap and torture Christian children, whose blood they drank for a variety of sinister purposes

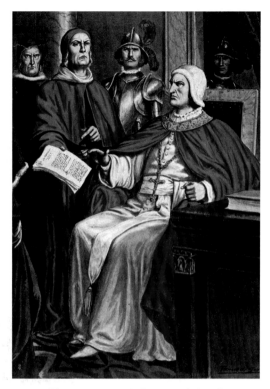

Pope Clement VI tried to explain that Jews also died from the plague, and thus could not be responsible for it, but his words did little to prevent violent anti-Semitism.

ranging from sadism and sorcery to the need, as unnatural beings, for Christian blood to give them a human appearance.[34]

To his credit, the reigning pope, Clement VI, tried to use simple logic to explain why Jews could not be guilty of causing the plague. He first pointed out that large numbers of Jews were dying of the disease. Why, he asked, would they knowingly kill many of their own kind? Moreover, the pope pointed out, numerous faraway lands in which no Jews lived had also been struck by the plague. So there had to be some other cause. Accordingly, Clement announced, no Christian should try "to capture, strike, wound, or kill any Jews."[35]

Unfortunately, anti-Semitism (prejudice against Jews) was so ingrained in Europe that very few people listened to or obeyed the pope. Huge numbers of Jews were horribly brutalized and massacred by angry mobs between 1348 and 1350. A surviving account by a German clergyman states that in the German town of Horw, all the Jews

were burned in a pit. And when the wood and straw had been consumed, some Jews, both young and old, still remained half alive. The stronger of [the Christians] snatched up [clubs] and stones and dashed out the brains of those trying to creep out of the fire.[36]

Sometimes Jews confessed to poisoning wells after being subjected to horrendous tortures. According to a surviving document, one Jewish man who was tortured in Switzerland was forced to confirm a scenario in which he carried "some prepared poison and venom in a thin, sewed leather-bag. [I planned to] distribute it among the wells, cisterns, and springs about Venice and the other places to which you [Christians] go, in order to poison [you]."[37]

Although the confession was untrue, it and others like it gave townspeople across Europe another convenient excuse to slaughter Jews. The following account from the German town of Strasbourg tells how the local Jews were burned alive in February 1349:

They burned the Jews on a wooden platform in their cemetery. There were about two thousand of them. Those who wanted to baptize themselves [as Christians] were spared. Many small children were taken out of the fire and baptized against the will of their fathers and mothers. And everything that was owed to the Jews was cancelled.... The [town] council, however, took the cash that the Jews possessed and divided it among the working-men proportionately.... After this wealth was divided among the artisans, some gave their share to the Cathedral or to the Church on the advice of their confessors. [In] some towns they burnt the Jews after a trial, in others without a trial. In some cities the Jews themselves set fire to their houses and cremated themselves [to deny their tormentors the satisfaction].[38]

Modern scholars estimate that in the span of only two to three years, at least sixty large Jewish communities were destroyed in Europe. About 150 smaller ones were exterminated as well. Moreover, an additional 350 or so cold-blooded massacres of Jews were witnessed and proudly recorded by Christian chroniclers.

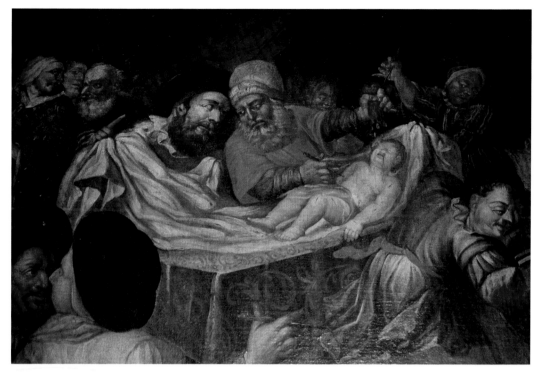

The blood libel was a medieval myth that Jews used the blood of ritually murdered Christian babies, depicted here, for evil purposes.

Weird Public Displays

Thus, many people attempted to combat the Black Death by imposing sanitation ordinances, restricting travel, and hounding and murdering innocent Jews and other scapegoats. When these acts failed to stop the epidemic, others appealed directly to God. But when the plague continued, they soon came to feel that their prayers were being ignored.

Some of the most devout Christians joined groups of flagellants, a name that comes from the word *flagellate*, meaning to punish by whipping. This name was well chosen. Groups of a few hundred and at times a few thousand flagellants traveled from town to town. When they reached the city center, they stripped themselves to the waist and beat themselves with whips until they bled. Bleeding was inevitable because these were no ordinary whips. According to an eyewitness, Heinrich of Herford, such a whip, called a scourge, was

a kind of stick from which three tails with large knots hung down. Through the knots were thrust iron spikes as sharp as needles, which penetrated about the length of a grain of wheat or a little more beyond the knots. With such scourges they beat themselves on their naked bodies so that they became swollen

Some devoted Christians became flagellants, meaning they would whip themselves in punishment as an appeal to God. They felt that their prayers for relief from the Black Death had been ignored.

and blue, and blood ran down to the ground and spattered the walls of the churches in which they scourged themselves.[39]

These beatings were supposed to dramatize the whippings Jesus received prior to his crucifixion. The intent was to sway God enough that he might forgive humanity's sins and halt the Black Death.

This first session of self-flogging was only the beginning of a typical flagellant ceremony. Next the worshippers sang dirges (mournful songs), including one with these words: "Our journey's done in the holy name. Christ Himself to Jerusalem came. His cross He bore in His holy hand. Help us, Savior of all the land." Sometimes they marched in circles, continuing to beat themselves and singing, "Come here for penance good and well, thus we escape from burning hell!"[40]

After that, it was common for the flagellants to lie down on the ground. Two of

The Flagellants' Sermon

The so-called Flagellants' Sermon was a prepared recitation that occurred near the end of the flagellants' morbid public spectacle of self-inflicted pain. It reads,

> Whoever to save his soul is fain, must pay and render back again. His safety so shall he consult. Help us, good Lord, to this result [and] ply well the scourge [spiked whip] for Jesus's sake, and God, through Christ, your sins shall take.... Woe! Usurer [lender who takes advantage of borrowers] though your wealth abounds, for every ounce you make, a pound shall sink you to the hell profound. You murderers and you robbers all, the wrath of God on you shall fall. Mercy you never to others show, [so] none shall you find, but endless woe.

Quoted in J.F.C. Hecker, *The Black Death*. London: Cassell, 1888, p. 65.

their number, called "masters," then walked back and forth among them, thrashing them with scourges or rods and reciting, "By Mary's honor free from stain, arise and do not sin again."[41] Obeying this order, the men on the ground stood up and began beating themselves again. Finally, they knelt before a large cross (representing the one on which Jesus was crucified) and listened as one of the masters recited the so-called flagellants' sermon, which warned society's sinners that God would sooner or later punish them.

At first, many of the townsfolk who watched this weird public display either sang along with the self-mutilators, wept for them, or both. Over time, however, most did not react and many ignored the flagellants and went about their business. This was because priests, both local ones and their leaders in Avignon, came to feel that the strange worshippers were usurping the clergy's main role as intermediary between God and humans. Churchmen were particularly upset when the flagellants began hearing people's confessions and granting them forgiveness for their sins. Also, in some towns the flagellants threw stones at local priests who tried to get them to leave, attempted to seize control of churches, and even stole expensive candlesticks and other items from church altars.

Perceiving the flagellants as a threat, clergymen and town leaders eventually combined forces against them. In October 1349 Pope Clement issued a decree ordering the arrest of flagellants. Influential churchmen made speeches in which they said the self-torturers were not inspired by God, as they claimed. At the same time, wealthy nobles had their knights and other soldiers hunt down and kill many flagellants. As a result of these efforts, the latter steadily disbanded. By the mid-1350s, a writer of that era colorfully noted that a majority of the flagellants had disappeared, "vanishing as suddenly as they had come, like night phantoms or mocking ghosts."[42]

Europe's Wreckage

Neither the flagellants, nor the priests, nor the town leaders, nor the nobles, nor, in fact, anyone was able to stop, or even slow down, the Black Death. It continued killing people and animals and disrupting societies and nations until, by the early 1350s, it had run its course. Modern scholars think it is possible that as many as 75 million of the estimated 500 million people then inhabiting the planet died from this single epidemic. That amounts to a staggering 15 percent of the human race.

But there seems to be little doubt that the overall devastation in Europe was particularly crippling. Pope Clement's agents and their contemporary, French writer Jean Froissart, estimated that a third of the continent's inhabitants were wiped out. Modern researchers generally agree. One leading expert on the onset of the plague in that era, Otto Friedrich, sums up Europe's wreckage this way:

> The chronicles of the fourteenth century [present] an image of deserted cottages falling in ruins and untilled wheat fields reverting to wilderness. Thousands of villages all across the face of Europe did simply disappear. The buried remnants are faintly visible in aerial photographs, spectral outlines of a vanished people, and in England alone more than two thousand such ruins have been recorded. The Germans even have a word, *Dorfwustungen*, for the process of villages turning into wilderness. The depopulation of the cities was no less remarkable. [In fact], virtually no city anywhere regained its population of [the year] 1300 in less than two centuries.[43]

Chapter Three

The Facts About the Plague

During the great outbreak of the plague in Europe and neighboring regions in the 1300s, three main facts were widely noted. First, large numbers of people were dying every day from a terrifying disease. Second, although many theories were advanced to explain the cause of the pestilence, no one knew the cause for sure. Third, as a result of the second fact, doctors were unable to stop the disease's spread, much less to cure it.

The modern world also has a set of facts relating to the contagion that ravaged Europe in the fourteenth century. Fortunately for humanity, the modern facts are both more numerous and more informative. This is primarily because of the rise of modern science beginning in the 1600s and 1700s. In addition to other modern marvels, scientists introduced the germ theory of disease in the 1800s. They demonstrated that tiny microbes, or germs, which are invisible to the unaided eye, can and often do invade people's bodies, causing a host of diseases.

This momentous revelation triggered widespread research, which over the years identified hundreds of diseases, including the one that caused the Black Death. A majority of medical researchers and historians agree that the main culprit in that horrendous epidemic was bubonic plague, a disease caused by bacteria. In his book, *The Black Death and the Transformation of the West*, scholar David Herlihy provides a thumbnail sketch of the breakthrough research on that ailment in the 1890s:

> Most notably in 1894, in China, the plague emerged from the inland provinces [and attacked] the port city of Hong Kong. [A] Swiss microbiologist named Alexandre Yersin . . . was then serving in the French colonial service in Indo-China. He hurried to Hong Kong and set up a

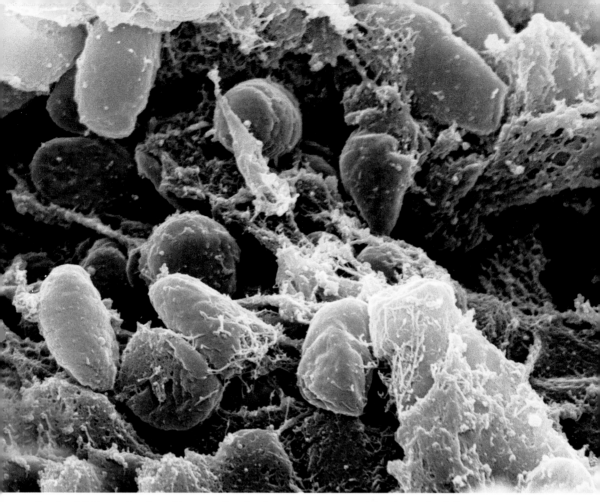

In the 1800s, scientists discovered microbes, or germs, and by the end of the century identified Yersinia pestis, *the microbe causing bubonic plague.*

laboratory there, in hopes of containing the disease before it struck southeast Asia. In 1894, he isolated the bacillus [the plague germ] and went on to develop a serum for the treatment of plague. The disease is consequently called ... *Yersinia pestis,* after Alexandre Yersin.[44]

As time went on, researchers came to better understand bubonic plague's ecology, or the manner in which it appears, reproduces, and spreads. This allowed scientists and doctors to find ways for people to avoid catching the disease. Even when a person does contract it, medical authorities can keep it from spreading and becoming an epidemic. In addition, learning the real facts about the plague has answered some nagging questions raised by the onset of the Black Death in the 1300s. It is now clear, for example, why medieval doctors' treatments were ineffective and why some people contracted the disease while others they were in contact with did not.

The Theory of "Infection"

Contrary to popular opinion, not all medieval doctors were totally ignorant of what causes most disease. Two brilliant fourteenth-century Islamic scholars, Ibn Khatima and Ibn al-Khatib, proposed an early theory of what they called "infection." Although not precisely a germ theory like the one introduced in the nineteenth century by European scientists, the earlier version was partially correct and far ahead of its time. According to one modern medical historian:

> In the middle of the fourteenth century, [when the] "Black Death" was ravaging Europe … Ibn al Khatib of Granada composed a treatise in the defense of the theory of infection in the following way: To those who say, "How can we admit the possibility of infection while the religious law denies it?" we reply that the existence of contagion is established by experience, investigation, the evidence of the senses, and trustworthy reports. These facts constitute a sound argument. The fact of infection becomes clear to the investigator who notices how he who establishes contact with the afflicted [sick person] gets the disease, whereas he who is not in contact remains safe, and how transmission is effected through garments, vessels and earrings.

Ibrahim B. Syed, "Islamic Medicine: 1000 Years Ahead of Its Times," ed. Shahid Ashar, Islam for Today (website), www.islamfortoday.com/athar04.htm.

Waiting for the Right Moment

The first important fact about bubonic plague, or the bacterium dubbed *Yersinia pestis*, is that it is primarily a disease of rats and other rodents, not humans. Outbreaks in human populations, experts say, are secondary and much less common than those in animal, especially rodent, populations. Scientists have found that at any given time, a few rodents or other small creatures in a handful of remote, unpopulated wilderness areas have the disease. Most of the time, these infected animals, together making up what medical experts call a disease reservoir, have too few bacteria in their systems to kill them or to cause the illness to spread. So the plague in a sense lays low in these carriers. For a few years, decades, or in some cases centuries, it remains trapped and dormant in its reservoir, as if waiting for an opportune moment to escape.

On occasion, evidence shows, the plague germs living in one or more wild

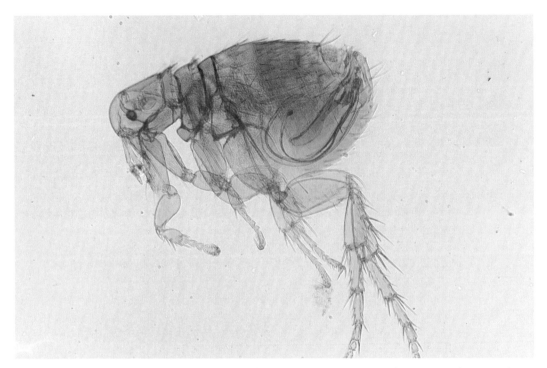

The rat flea was discovered to be a carrier for the plague, jumping from animal to people, consuming their blood, and spreading the disease.

animals become numerous enough to begin transferring from one animal to another. The means of transference, or vector, is usually fleas that normally live in animal fur. Most common among them is *Xenopsylla cheopis*, the rat flea. Some of the fleas consume their hosts' blood, which contains plague bacteria. The germs have little or no effect on the fleas but do manage to spread when a carrier flea lands on, bites, and infects a formerly uninfected animal. The process rapidly repeats itself, and the result can be an epizootic, an epidemic among wild creatures.

If the infected animals remain isolated from human civilization, the disease will run its course and once more begin to lay low in the local animal population. However, sometimes a different scenario takes place, one troubling and possibly scary for humans. As scholar James C. Giblin explains, this is how, in the 1300s bubonic plague most likely spread from rodents in remote sections of central Asia to people, perhaps hunters and traders who happened to pass through infested areas:

Although it was only an eighth of an inch long, the rat flea was a tough, adaptable creature. It depended for nourishment on the blood of its host, which it obtained through a dagger-like snout that could pierce the rat's skin. And in its stomach the flea often carried thousands of the deadly bacteria that caused the bubonic plague.... A black rat could tolerate a moderate amount of [the germs] without showing ill effects. But sometimes the flea contained so many bacteria that they invaded the rat's lungs or nervous system when the flea injected its snout. Then the rat died a swift and horrible death, and the flea had to find a new host. Aiding the tiny flea in its search were its powerful legs, which could jump more than 150 times the creature's length. In most instances the flea landed on another black rat. [But] if most of the rats in the vicinity were already dead or dying from the plague, the flea might leap to a human being [who happened to be nearby] instead.[45]

The Classic Symptoms

Having made the fateful jump to a person, the hungry flea immediately bit its new host. The hunter, trader, or other person perhaps felt a slight pinch, not realizing that it signaled the initial attack of an invisible but deadly invasion force. During the feeding process, the insect transferred some plague germs into the bite wound. The bacteria then made their way into the person's lymph system and from there to the lymph nodes. (These organs contain cells that help the body's immune system fight foreign invaders, including germs.)

The *Yersinia pestis* germs found the lymph nodes to be ideal places to multiply.

Soon they created colonies that increased in size until, within three to eight days, they became lumps the size of eggs or even small apples. These were the so-called buboes that numerous medieval writers mentioned when describing the classic symptoms of the Black Death. Most often the buboes appeared in the underarms or the groin.

After a couple more days had passed, the germs reached the victim's bloodstream. That allowed them to invade the vital organs, including the lungs and spleen. Soon dark spots appeared on the skin and in many cases blood oozed from the skin as well. Next, Giblin says, "the nervous system started to collapse, causing dreadful pain [in the limbs] and bizarre movements of the arms and legs. Then, as death neared, the mouth gaped open and the skin blackened from internal bleeding."[46] Finally came death, in a morbid way a sort of blessing to the pain-wracked, delirious victim.

Then the next phase in the lethal plague ecology ensued. Just as the infected fleas had earlier jumped off their dead rat hosts, they now left behind their dead human ones. Still loaded down with *Yersinia pestis*, they hopped madly about, searching for, and sometimes finding, a new human host. From hunters and traders to sailors, city dwellers, farmers, and others, the rampant germs ravaged one host after another.

Most modern experts are reasonably certain that the Black Death was bubonic plague that followed this general scenario. The primary evidence they cite to support this view is that many medieval

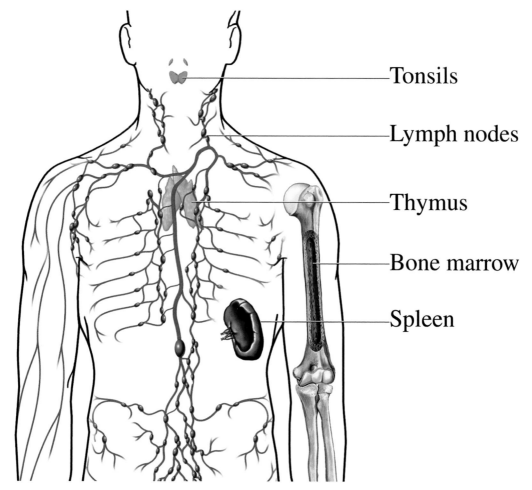

Plague bacteria mutiply in the lymph nodes, a part of the lymphatic immune system, and from there enter the bloodstream.

writers described symptoms identical or at least very similar to those seen in modern cases of plague. In fact, several of these classic symptoms were mentioned by Italian eyewitness Michael of Piazza in his description of the Black Death's great onset in the mid-1300s. He wrote:

Here not only the "burn blisters" appeared, but there developed gland boils on the groin, the thighs, the arms, or on the neck. At first these were of the size of a hazel nut, and developed accompanied by violent shivering fits, which soon rendered those attacked so weak that they could not stand up, but were forced to lie in their beds consumed by violent fever. Soon the boils grew to the size of a walnut, then to that of a hen's egg or a goose's egg, and they were exceedingly painful, and irritated the body, causing the sufferer to vomit blood. The sickness lasted three days, and on the fourth, at the latest, the patient succumbed. As soon as anyone in Catania [a town in Sicily] was seized with a headache and shivering, he knew that he was bound to pass away within the specified time.[47]

A Chain of Evidence

These medieval descriptions of the Black Death have long been of particular interest to epidemiologists, scientists who study disease epidemics. Epidemiologists are disease detectives who track down clues to the various ways that germs spread disease. For them, it was not enough to know how the plague bacteria made it out of a central Asian animal reservoir and infected some human passersby. It is obvious that those infected people proceeded to carry the contagion to one or more nearby towns. Epidemiologists wanted to know much more. They wanted to be able to trace, as best as they could, the course of the Black Death as it made its way through the Middle East and Europe. Piecing together this chain of evidence, so to speak, would help modern science better understand this killer disease and thereby keep it from unleashing new killer epidemics.

The Crimean port city of Kaffa became infected with the plague when attacking Mongols threw diseased corpses over the city's walls. The plague then spread from Kaffa to other cities on rats and fleas aboard ships.

Fortunately for medical researchers, one area of study often gathers information useful to others. Historians had started piecing together the crucial chain of evidence for the spread of the Black Death in the late nineteenth century. That chain begins in Kaffa, the Crimean port city that was besieged by the Mongols early in 1346. The residents of Kaffa were naturally concerned when the enemy started lobbing disease-ridden corpses over the city's walls. They were aware that these bodies were in some manner causing them to come down with a terrible sickness. But they had no idea how the disease was spreading among them. They had no clue that, like all disease epidemics, the one they were experiencing featured specific vectors, in this case paths of infection. Medical expert Alfred J. Bollet explains,

The corpses catapulted over the walls of Kaffa may not have been carrying competent plague vectors. Rats were not catapulted, but the city must have had its own supply [of rats]. The cadavers [dead bodies] may still have had infected fleas on them (either human or rat fleas, or both) and could thus have spread the disease inside the besieged city, or the infection could have been spread by [flea-infested] rats migrating into and out of the city despite the siege.[48]

Indeed, rats proved to be one of the two key vectors for the spread of the

Doctors Who Would Not Visit the Sick

Many medieval doctors died of the bubonic plague during the great outbreak known as the Black Death. The fact that they had no knowledge or ability to stop the epidemic was a tremendous embarrassment to those doctors who survived. A distinguished French physician of that time, Gui de Chauliac, wrote with regret:

The plague [was] shameful for the physicians, who could give no help at all, especially as, out of fear of infection, they hesitated to visit the sick. Even if they did, they achieved nothing, and earned no fees, for all those who caught the plague died, except for a few towards the end of the epidemic who had escaped after the buboes had ripened.

Quoted in Edouard Nicaise, ed., *La Grande Chirurgie*. Paris: Alcan, 1890, p. 171.

Black Death beyond Kaffa. The other was people on whom one or more fleas had made a temporary home. True, it was the fleas that carried the actual plague germs. However, the fleas could not have made it out of the city and onto ships without rats and humans to carry them.

Of these two carriers, the rats were by far the most numerous, crucial, and ultimately lethal. Indeed, a major reason that the pestilence was able to spread from one city or country to another so quickly was that no one suspected that rats were carrying the contagion. After all, rats were practically everywhere. They and other rodents scrounged for food in farmers' fields and barns, grain supplies, houses, shops, ships, and elsewhere. People had long since accepted them as pesky but ever-present nuisances. Not for a moment did they suspect that the rats were carrying the awful malady from place to place.

As a result, no one took notice as a few infected rats, or some carrying infected fleas, crawled from docks onto ships. From Kaffa, the vessels bore these live carriers of the pestilence to ports near and far. Harbormasters in a city that had not yet encountered the disease often ordered the crews and passengers of newly arrived ships to stay onboard. This is what happened when Genoese ships from the east reached the southern Italian port of Messina. But the strategy of keeping potentially infected people from leaving the ships did not prevent the spread of the plague. The harbormasters "had no way of knowing," Giblin points out, "that the actual carriers of the disease had already left the ships. Under cover of night, when no one could see them, they [the infected rats] had scurried down the ropes that tied the ships to the dock and vanished into [the city]."[49]

Three Interwoven Diseases

Once the rats carrying the infected fleas entered Messina and other port cities, the next step in the plague's assault on Europe took place. Namely, some of the fleas hopped off the rats and found human hosts. In turn, a large percentage of those people contracted the disease. When those victims died, the fleas transferred either to other humans or to animals, thereby spreading the contagion in all directions.

For the people who became infected with the Black Death, the disease took three possible routes. The most common was the passage of *Yersinia pestis* through the body, producing the classic symptoms described above. Medical experts generally refer to this most typical form of the illness, which was fatal in about 50 to 60 percent of cases, as bubonic, named for the buboes that form in the lymph nodes.

In a minority of cases, however, the disease takes one of two other forms. The first is called pneumonic plague because it involves a rare kind of pneumonia. Sometimes, when an infected person is exposed to a sudden and sharp drop in temperature, the germs can move into the lungs. The victim rapidly develops a severe cough and soon starts spitting up bloody mucus. Because the mucus contains plague microbes, when it flies into the air or lands on nearby objects, it can infect other people or animals directly. It

Rats carrying infected fleas helped distribute three kinds of plague: bubonic, pneumonic, and septicaemic. The last two types are the most fatal.

is therefore extremely contagious and dangerous. Death occurs in 95 to 100 percent of cases.

The third and rarest form of the disease, septicaemic plague, occurs when a fleabite causes the bacteria to enter the bloodstream right away and in huge numbers. As they move through the body, the germs keep multiplying. Within hours they infect all areas of the body, resulting in death in at most a day after the initial infection. About septicaemic plague, which is always fatal, British scholar Philip Ziegler says:

The victim is dead long before buboes have had time to form. It is in this form of plague that *Pulex irritans*, the man-borne flea, has a chance to operate. So rich in bacilli is the blood of a sick man that the flea can easily infect itself and carry on the disease to a new prey without the need of a rat to provide fresh sources of infection. Septicaemic plague must have been the rarest of the three interwoven diseases which composed the Black Death, but it was certainly as lethal as its pneumonic cousin and it introduced yet another means by which the plague could settle itself in a new area and spread hungrily among the inhabitants.[50]

Immunity and Other Factors

It is important to emphasize that some people in the 1300s, as well as in outbreaks of the plague in later eras, were exposed to the disease but did not contract it. The Black Death seemed to kill randomly. Often it wiped out whole families or entire neighborhoods and villages. Yet in many other instances, people who had been in close contact with those who were infected did not contract the pestilence and survived.

Experts point to a number of reasons for this phenomenon. First, they say, as long as the version a person was exposed to was bubonic, there was usually no direct, person-to-person transmission. The main vector was infected fleas, so one's chances of getting sick depended on one's exposure to the fleas. Therefore, the disease spread more easily in areas with poor sanitation, to which more flea-ridden rats were attracted. Conversely, in those places where homes and streets were cleaner, more people escaped infection. Also, because the deadly fleas often inhabited animal fur, people who had little or no contact with animals were less likely to get sick. Similarly, people who lived in houses with sturdy, more or less airtight walls were better off because fewer rats and fleas could get in.

While a great many people were killed by the plague, some never caught it, even if they helped administer to the sick. Having a strong immune system may have prevented these people from becoming sick.

An even more important factor affecting the plague's ease of transmission was personal immunity. As historian Robert S. Gottfried points out, "in the Middle Ages [medieval times], active immunity was particularly important in determining the extent and intensity of an epidemic."[51] Modern medical researchers have found that, for a variety of reasons, some people have stronger immune systems than others. Thus, a person with strong immunity had a good chance of fighting off the infection, especially if the number of germs transmitted by a given flea was fairly low. As a result of all these factors, and others, some people who were directly exposed to others suffering from the Black Death did not catch it.

Treatments and Cures

Of course, if medieval physicians had known about these factors, as well as the fact that the plague was caused by germs infesting fleas, they might have been able to prevent, or at least slow, the disease's spread. However, the sad fact is that they were completely ignorant of the plague's causes and modes of transmission. Because modern doctors do know these facts, they can explain why attempts by their medieval counterparts to treat the illness failed.

The treatments of Greek physician Galen were often followed in the 1300s to treat plague victims.

Doctors working in the 1300s most often followed the cures and treatments advocated by the second-century ancient Greek physician and medical researcher Galen. He was important in his own day because he did extensive medical research when most other physicians did not. However, doctors in later ages, thinking his word was final on medical matters, did little or no research of their own. They blindly accepted his assertions that illness resulted from factors such as a person's personality traits, the temperature or "purity" of the air, and/or eating or drinking too much.

Accordingly, doctors faced with the Black Death told their patients they could avoid the contagion by moving to places where the air was drier and cooler. They also admonished people not to bathe. This, they said, was because bathing would open the pores and thereby allow "bad" air to enter their bodies.

As for treating those already sick with plague, some doctors prescribed bed rest and drinking plenty of fluids. This was good advice, although by itself it was not enough to cure a disease as dangerous as the plague. Unfortunately for patients, doctors more often bled patients. This consisted of opening one or more veins, especially those located near buboes, and allowing "tainted" blood to drain out into a pan. Needless to say this only made the patient weaker. Also common was opening and draining the buboes, not realizing that many bacteria still remained inside and continued to multiply.

The Supreme Ancient Medical Expert

Galen, the ancient physician whom medieval doctors most admired, was born in the Greek city of Pergamum in A.D. 130. He grew up to be a brilliant scholar and thinker and the leading medical practitioner in the Roman Empire. He studied and in many ways adhered to the ideas of eminent doctors who came before him, especially Hippocrates, the fifth-century B.C. Greek scholar who was later called the father of medicine. Like Hippocrates, Galen held that disease is a natural phenomenon rather than a divine punishment. He performed numerous experiments, including the dissection of pigs, dogs, and other animals. In addition, he turned out hundreds of medical treatises, of which about eighty still survive. It was these writings, along with Galen's reputation as the supreme Greco-Roman medical expert, that made him popular, even revered, by doctors and other educated people in medieval times. Not until the early seventeenth century did medical science begin to significantly surpass Galen's ancient medical achievements.

In a different approach, many physicians tried applying various substances to the buboes, including a widely popular mixture of tree resin, ground lily roots, and human excrement. Other patients were forced to drink powdered gold or other metals mixed with water, a toxic brew that was more likely to kill the patient than the plague germs. Finally, when all else failed, people turned to prayer. Whether or not this approach worked was and remains a matter of personal faith.

Today doctors and other medical professionals thankfully do not have to deal with bubonic plague very often. But when they do, they possess treatments that are effective in the vast majority of cases. (This is provided, of course, that the correct diagnosis is made in a timely manner.) The standard

When nothing else seemed to work to stop the plague, people turned to prayer.

treatment for the plague is to isolate the victim and then administer a strong antibiotic, such as streptomycin, to kill the bacteria.

At first glance, this may seem like an unusually simple solution to a major problem. But one must keep in mind that it took thousands of researchers working diligently over the course of more than a century to accumulate the medical facts that made that deceptively simple solution a reality. Everyone alive today can count themselves fortunate that they were born after, rather than before, the facts about the plague and other dreaded diseases came to light.

Chapter Four

Diverse Economic Effects

Quite often when people discuss the onslaught of the Black Death in the 1300s, they single out the high death toll. This is only natural. After all, the number of deaths was so extraordinarily high that it still challenges the imagination. However there is sometimes a tendency to assume that when the epidemic subsided, the survivors went on with their lives more or less as before. Those who had been poor serfs before the plague, for example, remained poor serfs afterward, and within a few years things got back to normal.

The reality is far different. The calamity that struck Europe was so immense that all aspects of life changed, some of them forever. Social classes and customs, literature, the arts, and religion were all impacted. But perhaps the greatest alterations, both in the short-term and long-term, were economic in nature. Deeply affected were the prices of food and other essential goods and services; the need for and importance of various occupations; relations between management and labor; and the very structure of society's main economic supports. These and other economic effects of the Black Death changed the way many people, especially the poor and oppressed, saw society. The economic changes were so profound that some scholars rank them among the factors that brought about the decline of medieval times and the rise of early modern Europe.

The Manorial System in Crisis

The biggest single economic change driven by the great epidemic was the decline of the medieval manorial system. That system revolved around the manor—the large house, outbuildings, and surrounding lands owned by a wealthy noble. The people who worked on a typical manor, called peasants, owed loyalty and certain duties to the

Cities and Buildings Laid Waste

Economic reverses and other adverse effects of the Black Death were not restricted to Europe. The extensive Islamic regions of the Middle East and North Africa were also devastated, as shown by a surviving account by a Muslim writer of the era, Ibn Khaldun.

> Civilization both in the East and West was visited by a destructive plague which devastated nations and caused populations to vanish. It swallowed up many of the good things of civilization and wiped them out.... Cities and buildings were laid waste, roads and way signs were obliterated, settlements and mansions became empty, and dynasties [family lines of rulers] grew weak. The entire inhabited world changed.... It was as if the voice of existence in the world had called out for oblivion and restriction and the world responded to its call. God inherits the earth and whoever is upon it.

Quoted in Michael Dols, *The Black Death in the Middle East*. Princeton, New Jersey: Princeton University Press, 1977, p. 67.

noble who owned it. That owner was usually referred to as a lord and those below his social class addressed him as "my lord." In exchange for the lord's giving them protection and a place to live, the peasants labored for him, usually for life. They either toiled in the fields, planting and harvesting, or did some other form of work.

The vast majority of these laborers were serfs, poor people who were in a sense attached to the estate on which they lived and worked. Technically they were free to leave and look for work somewhere else. But if they did so, they no longer had a reliable way to feed themselves. In leaving the manor, they

also lost the legal and military protection the lord of the manor had provided them. Thus, afraid they might not be able to find an equally safe situation elsewhere, most stayed put. They, their children, and their grandchildren remained serfs, thereby providing the cheap labor that made the manorial system possible.

Because the cheap labor of so many peasant-serfs propped up the manorial system, logic dictates that if large numbers of those workers were suddenly gone, that system would collapse. Indeed, that is exactly what happened as a result of the onslaught of the Black Death. The plague killed so many people that entire sections of Europe rapidly

The property owned by landowners was worked by serfs, who ploughed fields and took care of livestock. The high death rate from the plague decimated this source of cheap labor.

became sparsely populated. A majority of landed estates lost at least half, and sometimes three-quarters or more, of their workers. A French writer who lived through the disaster described the effects of depopulation on the large agricultural estates:

Many have certainly heard it commonly said how in one thousand three hundred and forty nine [the year 1349], out of one hundred [workers on a manor] there remained but nine. Thus it happened that for lack of people many a splendid farm was left untilled. No one plowed the fields, bound the cereals, and took in the grapes.[52]

Clearly many of the nobles who owned manors with extensive farmland and/or vineyards no longer had enough cheap laborers both to maintain their estates and to turn a large profit. At the same time, the surviving peasants inhabiting those domains now put an added burden on the owners. Many of these serfs, realizing they suddenly had some leverage, or bargaining power, demanded a new financial arrangement. Many insisted on and gained the right to rent or lease the lands on which they lived.

As a result of these combined factors, the nobles who had long run the manorial system now found themselves in an economic crisis. According to historian Robert S. Gottfried:

> The value of agricultural products began to fall, and it stayed low relative to that of industrial goods until the sixteenth century. At the same time, depopulation made agricultural workers scarce and, thus, much more valuable. Wages rose rapidly. [At] Cuxham Manor in England, a plowman who was paid 2 shillings a week in 1347 received 7 shillings in 1349, and 10 shillings [by] 1350. The result was a dramatic rise in standards of living for those in the lower [social classes]. Day laborers not only received higher wages, but asked for and got lunches of meat pies and golden ale.[53]

Those Uppity Commoners

Gottfried and other modern scholars base their findings on surviving documents from the era of the Black Death. Several of these writings describe what seemed to many people at the time to be a topsy-turvy world in which traditional values and prices abruptly underwent drastic change. In particular members of the upper classes found it disconcerting, and even disgraceful, that poorer folk arrogantly took advantage of their "betters." Suddenly not only agricultural laborers, but also commoners in a wide range of jobs in the towns and cities, were demanding and getting higher

Members of the lower classes, such as these peasant workers, were able to demand higher wages for their work because the plague had killed so many workers.

Inflated Religious Fees

In the wake of the Black Death there was widespread suffering and a greatly increased need for spiritual aid by commoners who had survived the epidemic. A number of priests and other churchmen took advantage of the circumstances by charging inflated fees. In November 1378 the archbishop of Canterbury wrote a letter to the bishop of London, complaining:

[Many priests in Canterbury] have been so infected with the sin of greed that, not satisfied with reasonable wages, they hire themselves out for vastly inflated salaries. And these same greedy and pleasure-seeking priests vomit out the enormous salaries with which they are stuffed.

Quoted in Rosemary Horrox, ed., *The Black Death.* Manchester, England: Manchester University Press, 1994, p. 311.

wages. Furthermore they were availing themselves of goods, services, and customs normally reserved for the well-to-do and social elite. In 1363 Italian chronicler Matteo Villani reported with disdain:

The common folk, both men and women ... would no longer labor at their accustomed trades, but demanded the dearest and most delicate foods for their sustenance; and they married at their will, while children and common women clad themselves in all the fair and costly garments of the [upper-class] ladies dead by that horrible death [the plague]. Thus, almost the whole city [Villani's hometown of Florence], without any restraint whatsoever,

rushed into disorderliness of life.... Men dreamed of wealth and abundance in garments and in all other things [and] the work of all trades and crafts rose in disorderly fashion beyond the double.[54]

Villani also gave the following examples of "uppity" members of the lower classes who demanded and got better wages and benefits:

Serving girls and unskilled women with no experience in service and stable boys want at least 12 florins per year, and the most arrogant among them 18 or 24 florins per year, and so also nurses and minor artisans working with their hands want three times [the] usual pay, and laborers on the land all want oxen and all seed, and want to work the best lands, and to abandon all other [lands and allow nature to reclaim them].[55]

Many miles to the north of Italy, in plague-ravaged England, the situation was no different. An English country gentleman named John Gower was appalled by the attitudes of the members of the lower classes. In 1375 he commented that the world had swiftly gone from bad to worse and added:

[A] shepherd and cowherd [can now] demand more for their labor than the master-bailiff [farm manager] was wont [likely] to take in days gone by. Labor is now at so high a price that he who will order his business aright must pay five or six shillings now for what cost him two in former times. [The] poor and small folk [have the audacity to] demand to be better fed than their masters.[56]

In addition some professions came to be more in demand after the plague struck than they had been before. During the plague years there was a major need for more gravediggers, doctors, and priests (to administer last rights to and bury the dead). On the one hand, this need attracted many poorly trained opportunists to these jobs. On the other, because few were willing to take said jobs, those who did take them were able to charge premium prices. An English writer of the period recalled the following about priests:

There was so great scarcity and rarity of priests that parish churches remained altogether unserved, [and] many chaplains and hired parish priests would not serve without excessive pay. The Bishop of Rochester [intervened and] commanded these [priests] to serve at the same salaries [as before], under pain of suspension.[57]

Maintaining Class Distinctions

People charging more for their services was not the only example of rising prices in the years following the Black Death. Because so many people, including artisans and other skilled workers, had died in the epidemic, far fewer people were left to produce standard goods. These included all manner of food, wine, fabrics, clothing, linens, pottery, metal utensils and weapons, building materials, and so forth.

From an economic standpoint, the creation of fewer goods made those goods that *were* produced more valuable. In turn, this contributed to a general inflation, or rise in the prices of goods and services, throughout society. This inflation "persisted until the last decades of the fourteenth century," writes historian David Herlihy. It indicated "that under the shock of [the] plague, production in town and countryside had fallen even more rapidly than the population."[58]

Most of the nobles and other well-to-do people could afford to pay the higher

Sumptuary laws limited displays of luxury from certain classes. Wealthy people, such as the woman at left, could wear more extravagent dress, while lower classes were restricted to more plain attire.

prices, of course, although they were by no means happy about it. One might assume that most members of the lower classes could not afford to buy the more expensive items. However, it must be recalled that large numbers of these workers had demanded and were now making more money. As Villani pointed out, many people who were not used to luxuries now ate "delicate foods" and wore "fair and costly garments."

The problem with this trend was that numerous upper-class citizens were used to having a monopoly on such comforts. They were loathe to see people they viewed as inferiors enjoying access to such luxury goods because it seemed to go against nature. "Conspicuous consumption by the humble threatened to erase the visible marks of social distinctions and to undermine the social order,"[59] one expert remarks.

Hoping to keep that clearly delineated class system intact, the nobles, who ran the governments across Europe, passed hundreds of sumptuary laws in the century following the Black Death. These were regulations designed to limit displays of luxury and extravagance. Women were forbidden to wear dresses that did not conform to a certain style, for instance; similarly, only certain types of food and drink could be served at weddings.

These statutes were written in such a way as to restrain members of the lower classes but not wealthy and aristocratic people. The obvious hope was that such laws would reinforce the boundaries between the social classes. But as has been true of most such laws passed in history, they did not work. The higher living standards of many commoners in the postplague years remained a fact of life for the remainder of the medieval era.

Oppressive Rules Lead to Trouble

In desperation, some national rulers and town governments tried to keep various social groups in their place by more blatant and forceful means. Some rules forbade peasants from leaving the manors on which they had been raised. Others kept commoners who worked in shops and other businesses from switching jobs. Still others placed caps on how much commoners could earn in various jobs and professions. The object of such rules, scholar Philip Ziegler explains,

was to pin wages and prices as closely as possible to a pre-plague

In 1358, French peasants revolted in what became known as the Jacquerie. They were protesting their treatment by the upper classes and demanding more freedoms.

figure and thus to check the inflation that [began during the years of the Black Death]. The government realized that this could never be achieved as long as laborers were free to move from one employer to another in search of higher wages and so long as employers were free to woo away laborers from their neighbors with [tempting] offers. By restricting the right of an employee to leave his place of work; by compelling him to accept work when it was offered to him; by forbidding the employer to offer wages greater than those paid three years before;

[and] by fixing the prices which butchers, bakers, and fishmongers could charge their customers, they hoped to re-create the conditions that pertained before the plague and maintain them forever.[60]

Those citizens who ignored these oppressive rules were taxed or fined, and some who failed to pay the fines were arrested. Such extreme measures often ended up affecting all but society's wealthiest members and were very unpopular. English chronicler Henry Knighton described such measures enacted in England in the late fourteenth century:

The laborers were so lifted up and obstinate that they would not listen to the King's [new rules, and] when it was known to the King that they had not observed his command[s], he levied heavy fines upon abbots, priors, knights, greater and lesser, and other great folk and small folk of the realm…. And afterwards the king had many laborers arrested, and sent them to prison; many withdrew themselves and went into the forests and woods; and those who were [caught] were heavily fined. Their ringleaders were made to swear that they would not take daily

A Rebellion in England

One of the largest peasant rebellions of the period immediately following the Black Death occurred in England in 1381. Tens of thousands of people marched on London and tried to see the king, Richard II. A local chronicler of the time, Henry Knighton, recalled:

They directed their way to the Tower [of London] where the king was surrounded by a great throng of knights, esquires, and others [attempting to protect him]…. They [the peasants] complained that they had been seriously oppressed by many hardships and that their condition of servitude was unbearable, and that they neither could nor would endure it longer. The king, for the sake of peace, and on account of the violence of the times, yielding to their petition, granted them a charter … to the effect that all men in the kingdom … should be free and of free condition.

Quoted in Leon Bernard and Theodore B. Hodges, eds., *Readings in European History*. New York: Macmillan, 1958, pp. 214–15.

wages beyond the ancient custom, and then were freed from prison. And in like manner was done with the other craftsmen in the boroughs and villages.[61]

Such attempts to regulate wages and maintain the old social order through strong-arm tactics only further inflamed peasants and other commoners who already resented being held down. The result was a series of uprisings of workers that foreshadowed the larger anti-aristocratic revolutions that would rock Europe in the 1700s and 1800s. Probably the best-known example in the 1300s occurred in France in 1358. It was called the "Jacquerie" because French peasants were often called "Jacques." The French chronicler Jean Froissart recorded the following:

[A large number of enraged peasants] gathered together without any other counsel [leaders], and without any armor [except for] staves and knives, and so went to the house of a knight dwelling thereby, and broke up his house and slew the knight and the lady and all his children great and small and burned his house. And they then went to another castle, and took the knight thereof and bound him fast to a stake, and then violated his wife and his daughter before his face and then slew the lady and his daughter and all his other children, and then slew the knight by great torment and burned

and beat down the castle. And so they did to diverse other castles and good houses; and they multiplied so that they were six thousand [rebels], and ever as they went forward they increased [in number], so that every gentleman fled from them and took their wives and children with them ... and left their house void and their goods therein. These mischievous people thus assembled without captain ... robbed, burned, and slew all gentlemen that they could lay hands on, [and] did such shameful deeds that no human creature ought to think on any such, and he that did most mischief was most praised [by the others]. I dare not write the horrible deeds that they did.[62]

A similar large peasant revolt occurred in England in 1381. There, the reigning king, Richard II, felt so threatened that he gave the peasants a charter, or legal agreement, granting them a number of rights and freedoms they had never before possessed. Later that year, however, the king and his nobles canceled this agreement. Still, England's lower classes made some considerable gains in the course of the negotiations. The government had to reduce taxes and in the years to come it did not try to pass any laws designed to keep the wages of ordinary laborers low. As a result of these developments, by 1400 England's traditional manorial system had vanished from most parts of the kingdom.

From Rich to Poor

Historians note many other economic effects of the plague's fourteenth-century assault on Europe. One of the most interesting and rarely talked about is a decrease in the number of rich landowners in some areas. This is perhaps not surprising considering that the main source of income on many large estates—peasant workers—had been decimated by the Black Death. German scholar Friedrich Lutge sums up this trend, saying that as a result of the plague

> numerous peasant [land plots] were no longer occupied. Where they *were* occupied, the peasant was able to lessen his obligations [to the lord of the manor] in many ways because he was in high demand. There was, moreover, a decline in the purchasing power of money.... Thus, [some of] the landlords became impoverished [and] the German knightly order was reduced to bankruptcy. [A suddenly destitute noble often] took service, usually in a military or administrative capacity, with nobles who were still prosperous.[63]

This is another reminder of how the plague struck indiscriminately. Not only did it kill some people while leaving others untouched, it also created an economic situation in which even some of the rich could not escape its wrath.

Chapter Five

A Host of Cultural Impacts

In addition to the immediate and longer-lasting economic effects of the Black Death, Europe sustained what might be described as a huge blow to its psyche. Here the term *psyche* is defined as people's collective sense of who they are and how they should conduct their lives. Indeed, the various cultural aspects that made up people's lives had all been severely shaken by the plague's terrible visitation. Among these elements were learning, education, and literature; the arts and architecture; technology and science, including medicine; and religious faith and worship. This is only a partial list of the cultural aspects affected. As researcher Otto Friedrich says, the extermination of a large part of the human race must have affected people's outlook on life in profound ways, "and theories about the indirect effects of the Black Death touch on almost every aspect of life."[64]

From Optimism to Pessimism

Among the more immediately visible aspects of life that changed after the Black Death were communication skills and social manners and behaviors. All changed for the worse according to many medieval writers. Some of the most overt and troubling examples were obviously temporary. For instance, the Italian writer Giovanni Boccaccio described various episodes of antisocial behavior that occurred at the height of the epidemic. These included brothers abandoning brothers, priests fleeing their pulpits, and criminals running amok largely unchecked. However, later observers pointed out that these shameful acts were part of a sort of mass hysteria generated by the immediate danger of mass death and were widespread only in the short-term. After the great outbreak of pestilence ran its course, they say, such extreme behaviors became rare.

Italian author Giovanni Boccaccio wrote about antisocial behavior that took place at the height of the plague, such as family members abandoning one another.

Still, a number of Boccaccio's contemporaries mentioned what they felt were more permanent changes in manners in the following years. French monk and chronicler Jean de Venette said that a number of people displayed what he saw as too much coarseness, thoughtlessness, and selfish behavior:

After [the] cessation of the epidemic, pestilence, or plague, the men and women who survived married each other [and had a new generation of children]. But woe is me! The world was not changed for the better but for the worse by this renewal of population. For men were more [greedy] than before, even though they had far greater possessions. They were more covetous and disturbed each other more frequently with [law] suits, brawls, [and other] disputes. [Moreover] the enemies of the king of France and of the Church were stronger and wickeder than before and stirred up wars on sea and on land. Greater evils than before [swarmed] everywhere in the world.[65]

It is difficult to know how much of this tirade is based on real, continent-wide changes in social attitudes and manners and how much reflected mainly Venette's own local experiences. But evidence conclusively shows that life did not go back to normal after the epidemic of 1347–1351. No sooner had fear of the plague begun to subside than several more outbreaks of the same disease swept Europe in the second half of the century. Although smaller than the initial outbreak, these new threats seemed to have discouraged many people and hardened them toward life, which they came to see as uncertain and cruel. As historian Robert Gottfried puts it, "much of the cruelty and violence [of] the late fourteenth and fifteenth centuries can be understood only by keeping in mind the new [almost constant presence] of plague and the possibility of sudden, painful death." He adds that before the Black Death, European literature and art "expressed a buoyant optimism" (a hopeful outlook) about life. In contrast, "after the Black Death, this was replaced by a pervasive pessimism,"[66] or a gloomy, mistrustful outlook.

The Dance of Death

Some experts speculate that at the core of this new pessimistic view of human existence was a more gruesome and fatalistic way of looking at the concepts of life and death. As always, the vast majority of people clung to life and hoped for longevity and success. But now, more than before, thanks to the plague's periodic assaults, they recognized the inevitability of death, which seemed to lurk menacingly around the nearest corner. The chief image of this new outlook was the macabre, or ghastly and ghoulish, visage of the walking, talking skeleton. Artists, sculptors, and writers alike frequently used this likeness. Often they showed or described one or more skeletons dancing, a morbid, frightening

During the plague, people took on a darker outlook. Death was imagined as a walking, talking skeleton. One or more skeletons together would engage in a "dance of death."

scene that became known as the "danse macabre," or dance of death.

A widespread, grisly fascination for that chilling image spread all across Europe in the late 1300s and early 1400s. As the noted Dutch historian Johan Huizinga explains, there was a "desire to invent a visible image of all that [was concerned with] death." There was a particular attraction for "the cruder conceptions of death," which "impressed themselves continually on [people's] minds." It was not just regret over those struck down by the plague that motivated this fixation on such terrifying images. Rather, it was the fear of one's own death, and this [was] only seen as the worst of evils. Neither the conception of death [nor] that of a rest long wished for, of the end of [earthly] suffering [had] a share in the funereal [death-obsessed] sentiment of that [age]. The dominant thought [was] of death [as being very close], hideous, and threatening.[67]

The dance of death and other dark, morose interests were part of a larger view of a changed world in which the general consensus was that the traditional fixed

"On All Sides Is Sorrow"

The onset of the Black Death inspired many Europeans to express their horror or sorrow in writing. Some of these accounts later came to be seen as pieces of literary art, an outstanding example being this letter penned by the Italian writer Petrarch to his brother, a monk:

Alas! my beloved brother, what shall I say? How shall I begin? Whither shall I turn? On all sides is sorrow; everywhere is fear. I would, my brother, that I had never been born, or, at least, had died before these times. How will posterity believe that there has been a time when without the lightnings of heaven or the fires of earth, without wars or other visible slaughter, not this or that part of the earth, but well-nigh the whole globe, has remained without inhabitants. When has any such thing been even heard or seen; in what annals has it ever been read that houses were left vacant, cities deserted, the country neglected, the fields too small for the dead and a fearful and universal solitude over the whole earth?

Quoted in Decameron Web, "Petrarch on the Plague," Decameron Web (Web site), www.brown.edu/ Departments/Italian_Studies/dweb/plague/perspectives/petrarca.php.

order of things was in shambles or somehow out of whack. Some people speculated that God had imposed this catastrophic situation because he was angry about human failings and sins. But a number of other people felt the disaster was too big to be explained by God alone. There had to be some other factor, one that was perhaps beyond human comprehension. In the words of American historian Barbara W. Tuchman:

God's purposes were usually mysterious, but this scourge [curse] had been too terrible to be accepted without questioning. If a disaster of such magnitude, the most lethal ever known, was a mere wanton act of God, or perhaps not God's work at all, then the absolutes of a fixed order were loosed from their moorings [underlying supports]. Minds that opened to admit these questions could never again be shut. Once people envisioned the possibility of change in a fixed order, the end of an age of submission came in sight. The turn to individual conscience lay ahead. To that extent, the Black Death may have been the unrecognized beginning of modern man.[68]

A Crisis of Faith

Thus, the way that most Europeans viewed death, God, and life in general had been permanently altered. One of the leading modern experts on the Black Death, Philip Ziegler, calls it "a crisis of faith." To support that assertion, he writes:

Assumptions which had been taken for granted for centuries were now in question, the very framework of men's reasoning seemed to be breaking up. And though the Black Death was far from being the only cause, the anguish and disruption which it had inflicted made the greatest single contribution to the disintegration of an age.[69]

The chief repository, or storehouse, of faith in that age, of course, was the Roman Catholic Church. So any reduction in faith permeating society naturally affected the way people viewed the church. Their outlook on and trust of priests and other clergy, the relationship between the individual person and God, and the universal fate that God was seen to control also came into question.

Because God was invisible and rarely, if ever, communicated directly with people, many fourteenth-century Europeans were unsure of the deity's role in the Black Death. However, members of the clergy were very visible, and their behavior during the crisis was well-known. First, many priests and bishops had died in the epidemic. So it was clear that, despite their close ties with God, they possessed no immunity to the disease. Some saw this as a strike against them. A second perceived failing was that the clergy had demonstrated an inability to persuade God to stop the plague and spare the millions who died. Third, and worst of all, numerous priests had simply abandoned their posts and left their parishioners to suffer and die.

The Black Death led people to question the faith they had placed in God and in the trust they had for clergy as their intermediaries to God. After all, they had not been able to talk to God and stop the plague.

In addition, some people felt that the pope, then based in Avignon, France, had not set a good example during the catastrophe. Rumors spread that instead of risking his life to help members of his flock, he went to extraordinary lengths to save himself. To some degree this was true. Aided by his personal physician, Pope Clement VI hid in his papal apartment for months. There, attendants kept large fires burning in an effort to ward off whatever evil forces people imagined were causing the contagion.

As a result of these failings, the church sustained a major blow to its once immense prestige in society. Following the outbreak of the Black Death, most Europeans continued to believe in God, and while some left the church, many decided to stay. However, large numbers of the faithful came to feel that priests were not the special individuals that most people had previously assumed they were and that the church was inherently flawed. Scholar James Giblin points out that, although the church remained a powerful social institution,

it never regained the complete authority it had enjoyed before the

A Half-Built Cathedral

One common cultural effect of the Black Death was that the labor shortages it created kept many large-scale buildings from being completed. One of the best-known examples is a cathedral in the Italian city of Siena, which was in the midst of construction when the Black Death arrived in the city in the late 1340s. The transept, or section crossing the main hall (nave) at a right angle, was already in place. Workmen had also laid the foundations of the nave and choir. Because so many workmen died during the epidemic, most of the rest of the project was abandoned. The rest of the half-built cathedral remained, however, and over time became an accepted part of the city, as well as a popular tourist attraction in modern times.

plague. Once people began to question the Church's actions, they kept on questioning them. This eventually led to attempts to reform the Roman Catholic Church and then, in the sixteenth century, to the establishment of the first Protestant churches.[70]

As the church steadily came to be seen more as a human-made, rather than God-made, institution, the daily and yearly religious habits and rituals of many Europeans began to change. In earlier times, it was common, even universal, for someone who felt troubled, worried, or lost to ask a clergyman to pray for him or her. But in the postplague era it became increasingly common for people to ask loved ones to do so, or to pray for themselves.

Also following the Black Death, Europe witnessed a major increase in charitable giving. Hospitals, poor people, and others perpetually in need of public support benefited from the upsurge in good works by the faithful. In addition, larger numbers of people than ever before took leaves of absence from their normal activities and went on long, frequently arduous pilgrimages to holy Christian shrines. Among the most popular were the church in England where Saint Thomas Becket had been murdered; the sites of Jesus's arrest, trial, and crucifixion in Jerusalem; Saint Peter's tomb in Rome; and Compostela, Spain, where several miracles had been said to occur.

Many scholars think these and numerous other good works that people performed in that era were ways for them to pacify and conciliate God. According to this view, the aim was to appease him as much as possible. Those who still believed in him hoped this would persuade him not to send any more destructive plagues to punish humanity.

Charitable giving increased after the Black Death. People also began to go on more pilgrimages to sacred places, such as St. Thomas Becket's Tomb in England and Compostela, Spain.

Advances in Technology and Medicine

Another important aspect of culture affected by the Black Death consists of new scientific knowledge, especially in the form of advances in technology. As Gottfried points out, "there was a direct relationship between technology and depopulation."[71] Before the advent of the plague in the mid-1300s, most work, especially various types of menial labor, was accomplished by hand with the aid of some simple tools. So when a large proportion of Europe's workers died in

the epidemic, there were no longer enough hands to do all the work that needed to be done.

One obvious and quick solution was to increase the number of existing work-saving devices. The result was that many new windmills and watermills were built in England, France, Netherlands, and elsewhere. Such devices were not capable of doing all of the diverse sorts of work required to keep society going, however. New kinds of devices were clearly needed, and thankfully, Gottfried continues, "shortage" proved to be "the mother of medieval invention." The sudden removal of millions of workers from society "put a premium on *new* techniques that could save work time."[72]

One good example cited by Gottfried and other experts is the fishing industry. Fish was an important part of people's diets in numerous European kingdoms. Before the great pestilence struck, fisherman routinely came ashore from time to time to salt, and thereby preserve, the fish they had recently caught. Then they sailed back out and caught more fish. The problem after the plague was that all these steps slowed down since there were fewer fishermen to do the work. So the number of fish that could be caught and preserved was too small to sustain people's needs. Driven to find solutions to this problem, "in 1380, Dutch fishermen perfected a method of salting, drying, and storing their catch aboard ship," Gottfried writes. "This allowed them to stay at sea longer, sail farther from shore, and bring home more fish."[73]

The First Printing Press.

The printing press was created because of the need to replace people who had copied manuscripts by hand.

The Triumph of Death

One of the most famous and stunning European artistic renderings inspired by the Black Death is a fresco (painting done on wet plaster) by the Italian master Francesco Traini in 1350. It is appropriately titled the *Triumph of Death*. Noted scholar Barbara W. Tuchman provides this vivid description of the work:

> In Traini's fresco, Death swoops through the air toward a group of carefree, young, and beautiful noblemen and ladies who ... converse and flirt and entertain each other with books and music in a fragrant grove of orange trees. A scroll warns that "No shield of wisdom or riches, nobility or prowess" can protect them from the blows of the Approaching One. [In] a heap of corpses nearby lie crowned rulers, a Pope in a tiara [crown], [and] a knight, tumbled together with the bodies of the poor, while angels and devils in the sky contend for the miniature naked figures that represent their souls. A wretched group of lepers, cripples, and beggars ... implore Death for deliverance.

Barbara W. Tuchman, *A Distant Mirror: The Calamitous 14th Century*. New York: Ballantine, 1996, p. 130.

An even more important technological advance spawned largely by the loss of a major portion of the work force during the epidemic was the invention of printing with movable type. Better known as the printing press, it instantly revolutionized the production, distribution, and consumption of literature and other written materials. Indeed, few inventions in history have transformed the world as much as this one did. Yet today it is not widely known that the printing press came about because there was a major need to replace the thousands of trained individuals who for many centuries had painstakingly copied manuscripts by hand. Historian David Herlihy explains:

The growth of universities in the twelfth and thirteenth centuries and the expanding numbers of literate laymen generated a strong demand for books. Numerous scribes were employed to copy manuscripts. At Paris, for example, in the [1200s], manuscripts were divided into [sections] and given to separate scribes, who assiduously reproduced them. The parts were then combined into the finished book. As long as wages were low, this method of reproduction based on intensive human labor was satisfactory enough. But the late medieval population plunge raised labor costs and also raised the premium to be claimed by the one who could devise a cheaper way of reproducing books. Johann Gutenberg's invention of printing on the basis of movable metal type in 1453 was only the culmination of many experiments carried on across the previous century. His genius was in finding a way to combine several technologies into the new art.[74]

Developing alongside of these and similar technical advances stimulated by the Black Death were increases in medical knowledge and techniques. People were painfully aware that their doctors had lacked the knowledge and ability to stop the plague. Later outbreaks of the disease in the late 1300s and early 1400s only served to drive home the dire need for advances in medical science.

Heeding this call to improve their craft, a number of European doctors admitted they did not know enough about the human body. To remedy this shortcoming, they began dissecting cadavers, a practice that had long been frowned on and banned. Such studies brought about major new advances in the emerging science of anatomy. There was also a new interest and confidence in direct surgical methods. European universities had failed to teach these in the preplague years, but several began adding surgical instruction in the century following the plague.

The Survival of Learning

The teaching of surgical methods was only one of many examples of how European higher education changed following the

Black Death. In the short run, one noticeable change was a sudden decrease in the number of qualified, learned instructors. Another was a drop-off in student attendance at most universities. This is not surprising, as both were to be expected in the immediate aftermath of so much social chaos and mass death.

Highly literate and educated people, who in those days made up only a small percentage of the population, were at first extremely concerned. Charles IV,

Holy Roman emperor Charles IV felt it was important to preserve knowledge that the plague risked eliminating. Several universities were founded in the plague's aftermath, including Trinity College and Cambridge University.

ruler of the central European realm known as the Holy Roman Empire, expressed a desire to save "precious knowledge which the mad rage of pestilential [disease-driven] death has stifled throughout the wide realms of the world."[75] He and others worried that universities, and perhaps learning itself, might not survive the devastation the plague had wrought. This motivated them to look for qualified replacements, where possible, for the lost teachers. Also, those who had the necessary resources established several new universities in the era following the Black Death. Among the more famous and long lasting were Trinity College, at Cambridge, England, and Charles's own pet project, the University of Prague.

The great plague epidemic may also have affected learning by making literature easier to read and more available to more people. Some modern scholars point out that before the Black Death teachers and priests (who copied and preserved many writings) used Latin for most documents; but the era after the plague witnessed a switch to writing in vernacular languages (popular local tongues like Italian, French, German, and English). Explaining this theory, historian William McNeill says that "the decay of Latin as a *lingua franca* [universal language] among the educated men of western Europe was hastened by the die-off of clerics [priests or other church officials] and teachers who knew enough Latin to keep that ancient tongue alive."[76]

If this theory is true, it is one more way that European culture, ideas, and values, which later spread across the globe, were shaped to no small degree by a killer disease.

Chapter Six

The Plague in Later Ages

The bubonic plague outbreak that struck Europe in the 1340s had largely ended by 1351, leaving at least a third of the continent's human population dead. Yet as it turned out, that great epidemic, which came to be called the Black Death, was not the last that Europeans would see of the disease. It was destined to return numerous times. All subsequent visitations were smaller than the initial one. But all took awful tolls, killing thousands, spreading fear, and devastating local economies.

Of course, at the time doctors and other authorities did not know what caused the disease, much less why it kept coming back. So there was nothing to be done except to hope it would not strike one's own region or town and to do one's best to endure it if and when it did strike. In contrast, people alive today do not have to worry about the plague. Fortunately for them, medical science made huge strides in the early modern era. One result was a basic understanding that most diseases are caused by germs. Another, more specific, result was the identification of the particular germ that causes bubonic plague. Thus, although the plague still exists, it no longer poses the enormous threat to individuals and society that it once did. This does not mean that it has been forgotten, however. The Black Death remains a potent reminder of the potential horrors of disease epidemics. Its memory also haunts popular culture as an everlasting symbol of God's wrath and of massive death tolls resulting from practically any cause.

A Deadly Plague Cycle

As massive death tolls go, that of the Black Death between 1347 and 1351 was undoubtedly one of the two largest in history. (The terrifying influenza outbreak of 1918–1920 may have killed 100 million people, 25 million more than

Plague in 1665.

The plague outbreak of 1347–51 is known as the Black Death, but the plague returned numerous times. England experienced regular bouts from the fourteenth to eighteenth centuries.

the estimated 75 million who died worldwide of the Black Death.) Nevertheless, the bubonic plague outbreaks that struck Europe in the centuries immediately following the Black Death were frightening and destructive in their own right.

The first major onset of the disease after the one that ended in 1351 appeared

a decade later. In 1361, what those who experienced it called the *pestis secunda*, or "second plague," arrived with a vengeance. "The return of plague was a nightmare reborn," historian Robert Gottfried writes.

> While primarily an attack of bubonic plague [alone, with very little evidence of the pneumonic variety], and not as severe as the Black Death, the *pestis secunda* was still one of the most lethal epidemics in history. Many observers … believed it was especially deadly for select groups, including the young—those born after the Black Death [who had no immunity]—and the landed upper classes.[77]

Indeed, accounts of the disaster by eyewitnesses suggest that at least a quarter of the nobles in England were wiped out by the second bout of plague. The same outbreak seems to have killed about 20 percent of the peasant workers in Normandy, in northwestern France; close to a hundred thousand people in Florence, Italy; and overall at least 10 percent of Europe's population.

After that, the contagion seemed to just keep on coming. Every few years it reappeared, sometimes in one country, other times in several, forming a recurring pattern that later experts dubbed a "plague cycle." England, for instance, was hit in 1369, 1381–1382, 1387, 1405–1406, 1411–1412, 1426, 1428–1429, and several other times in the three centuries that followed.

Disease Caused by Earthquakes?

Well after the terrible bubonic plague outbreak of the 1300s, smaller epidemics of the disease struck Europe. Most people continued to accept outmoded, nonsensical theories about the causes of these epidemics. One of the most common theories was that earthquakes were the culprit. Although this seems silly today, at the time people were just as ignorant about the causes of earthquakes as they were about the causes of disease epidemics. One common explanation for earthquakes was that they happened when dangerous fumes trapped beneath the earth suddenly belched to the surface. These same fumes, which were supposedly "corrupt" in some way, were thereby released into the atmosphere, where they caused diseases, including the Black Death.

Although none of these outbreaks produced the gigantic death toll the Black Death had, the despair and suffering of those families affected by the sickness were no less intense. During a 1471 outbreak in England, a man visiting London sent a letter to his relatives in Norfolk. He wrote, "I pray you send me word if any of our friends or well wishers be dead, for I fear that there is great death [in] Norfolk, for I assure [you] that this is the most universal death that I ever witnessed in England."[78]

The enormity and horror of this seemingly relentless cycle of death by plague in Europe can be seen in various surviving statistics. Northern Germany had 179 local villages in 1300, before the first onset of plague, for example. In 1500, after numerous outbreaks of the disease in the region, only 33 of those villages still existed. The rest had been totally wiped out by the disease.

No less terrifying a statistic came from late medieval Italy. More than a million people died there in an outbreak of plague that struck in 1630–1631 alone.

Why the Plague Subsided

Major outbreaks of bubonic plague eventually slowed, and the disease became considerably less lethal. This was due to a series of events that happened over time, some of which remain somewhat controversial. In 1720 in what is now Hungary, for example, hundreds of checkpoints were set up and manned by thousands of guards. These acted as a rudimentary quarantine by limiting traders and other human traffic moving into Europe from the east. Also, some researchers have suggested that brown rats replaced black rats in many regions. Because brown rats tend to have less contact with people, the theory proposes, fewer infected fleas reached

*Doctors treating later epidemics of plague
began to wear protective clothing, as shown
in this seventeenth century depiction.
Many factors contributed to controlling
outbreaks, including checkpoints that
restricted travel, and most importantly,
the discovery of germs.*

human populations. A third suggested
reason for the subsidence of plague in
Europe is that the original bacteria that
caused the disease evolved into a less
deadly form.

Still another factor that must not be
overlooked is the nineteenth-century
discovery that germs cause disease. Also
crucial was identification of the microbe
that causes plague. Coupled with better
sanitary practices in much of Europe in

the nineteenth century, scientific knowledge definitely helped to reduce the
death toll from many harmful diseases,
including plague.

The key period in which many of these
breakthroughs were made began in 1854.
That was the year in which French scientist
Louis Pasteur demonstrated that germs
cause the process of fermentation (as in
grape juice fermenting into wine). Scientists knew about the existence of germs
before that. But they had assumed that
these tiny creatures played no major role,
harmful or otherwise, in nature. In his experiments with fermentation, Pasteur
showed that this was not the case.

Next, Pasteur and some other scientists set out to confirm something they
already suspected—that germs also
cause disease. In those days most people,
including a number of leading scientists,
found this idea difficult to accept. This
was partly because such notions went
against centuries of accepted medical
tradition.

Pasteur selected anthrax, a deadly disease common in cattle and sheep, to test
the germ theory. First, he made an anthrax
vaccine by heating anthrax spores—a
form of the germ that has not yet ma-
tured into an adult and lethal anthrax
bacterium. The heat weakened the
spores. When he injected them into some
lab animals, the creatures appeared to
become immune to anthrax.

This was not enough to convince the
scientists who disagreed that anthrax
bacteria and other germs cause disease.
They pushed Pasteur to do a larger experiment in public. On May 5, 1881, in a

village south of Paris, with both scientists and newspaper reporters watching, Pasteur and his assistants injected twenty-five sheep with their anthrax vaccine. Twenty-five other sheep standing nearby received no vaccine. The next step was to give the vaccinated sheep a few weeks to build up immunity. Finally, on May 31 Pasteur injected all fifty sheep with full-strength, mature anthrax germs.

Many people, including Pasteur's critics, expected nothing out of the ordinary to happen to the sheep. But on June 2, all of the unvaccinated sheep died of anthrax, while all of the vaccinated ones remained perfectly healthy. Pasteur had shown clearly that anthrax bacteria caused the disease and further, that a vaccine made from the same bacteria could make an animal immune from anthrax.

Scientists were inspired by Pasteur's experiment, and they began isolating and studying the germs that cause a number of harmful diseases. It was one of Pasteur's associates, Alexandre Yersin, who isolated the bubonic plague bacterium in 1894. Yersin also searched for specific vectors that might transfer the disease to humans but was unable to confirm any. Not long afterward, French

"I had Uncovered a Secret"

French scientist Paul-Louis Simond, who in 1898 established that the rat flea was the main carrier of bubonic plague, later recalled his excitement when the experiment confirming his suspicions worked.

Without delay I proceeded to the experiment I had in mind since the time ... when I had discovered Yersin's bacillus in the digestive tract of fleas taken from plague-ridden rats. I prepared [the materials and devices required for the experiment]. I was fortunate enough to catch a plague-infected rat in the home of a plague victim. In the rat's fur there were several fleas running around.... That day, 2 June 1898, I felt an emotion [of excitement that is hard to express] in the face of the thought that I had uncovered a secret that had tortured man since the appearance of plague in the world. The mechanism of the propagation of plague includes the transporting of the microbe by rat and man, its transmission from rat to rat, from human to human, from rat to human and from human to rat by parasites [fleas]!

Quoted in Marc Simond et al., "Paul-Louis Simond and His Discovery of Plague Transmission by Rat Fleas: A Centenary," *Journal of the Royal Society of Medicine*, February 1998, p. 102. Also available at www.ncbi. nlm.nih.gov/pmc/articles/PMC1296502/pdf/jrsocmed00028-0047.pdf.

Scientist Louis Pasteur's research showed that germs play a role in disease. This major scientific breakthrough helped control the damage of future plague outbreaks.

scientist Paul-Louis Simond, who worked at the Pasteur Institute in Paris, found that the principal vector was the rat flea.

Thanks in large part to Pasteur and other modern medical researchers, therefore, the plague no longer delivers misery and death as it did in past ages. However, it is important to point out that the disease still exists. This has been proven by occasional isolated incidents.

In 2003, for example, a couple from Santa Fe, New Mexico, decided to spend a few days in New York City. They did not know that they had recently been bitten by fleas carrying bubonic plague. After coming down with initial symptoms, including fever and fatigue, they checked into a local hospital, where it was found that the husband had developed an advanced stage of the disease. Thanks to the excellent medical care he received, both he and his wife survived. The husband, however, had to have both legs amputated below the knee.

Finding Meaning in Chaos

Another way the plague remains periodically in the public eye and human memory is in dramatic literary and artistic references to its former destructive power. The memory of the Black Death haunts popular culture as an everlasting symbol of God's wrath and of massive death tolls resulting from practically any cause. Indeed, in novels, plays, poems, lectures, paintings, and films, the Black Death often takes on almost supernatural qualities, as if it was a living, thinking being that had set out to haunt and terrorize humanity. "As the actual plague recedes into history," one modern researcher observes, "the memory of it becomes increasingly symbolic, like something from a dream, a subject for mythological interpretations."[79]

Modern thinkers, writers, and artists have repeatedly stressed the idea that even today's so-called advanced modern society must be modest enough to admit its limitations. Nature's wrath, like bubonic plague, is always lurking, waiting for its next chance to humble humanity. Only by continuing to explore nature and unlock its secrets can civilization escape the next Black Death–like catastrophe. In the words of the American historian William H. McNeill:

> Everyone can surely agree that a fuller comprehension of humanity's ever-changing place in the balance of nature ought to be part of our understanding of history, and no one can doubt that the role of infectious diseases in the natural balance has been and remains of key importance.[80]

Notes

Introduction: The Wild Cards of History

1. Giovanni Boccaccio, *Decameron*, trans. J.G. Nichols. New York: Knopf, 2009, pp. 8, 10.
2. Robert S. Gottfried, *The Black Death: Natural and Human Disaster in Medieval Europe*. New York: Macmillan, 1985, pp. 134–35.
3. Isaiah 37:33–36.
4. William H. McNeill, "Infectious Alternatives: The Plague that Saved Jerusalem," in Robert Cowley, ed., *What If: The World's Foremost Military Historians Imagine What Might Have Been*. New York: Berkley, 1999, p. 9.
5. Cowley, *What If*, p. 2.
6. Thucydides, *The Peloponnesian War*, trans. Rex Warner. New York: Penguin, 1972, pp. 152–153.
7. Procopius, *History of the Wars*, trans. H.B. Dewing. Cambridge, MA: Harvard University Press, 1935, pp. 451–452
8. Gabriel de Mussis, *Historia de Morbo*, excerpted in Rosemary Horrox, ed., *The Black Death*. Manchester, England: Manchester University Press, 1994, pp. 14, 16.

Chapter One: Onset of the Black Death

9. Alfred J. Bollet, *Plagues and Poxes: The Impact of Human History on Epidemic Disease*. New York: Demos, 2004, p. 20.
10. Quoted in Horrox, *The Black Death*, p. 17.
11. Philip Ziegler, *The Black Death*. New York: Harper Perennial, 2009, p. 5.
12. Quoted in David Herlihy, *The Black Death and the Transformation of the West*, ed. Samuel K. Cohn Jr. Cambridge, MA: Harvard University Press, 1997, p. 24.
13. Quoted in Johannes Nohl, *The Black Death*, trans. C.H. Clarke. Yardly, PA: Westholme, 2006, pp. 18–19.
14. Quoted in Nohl, *The Black Death*, p. 18.
15. Boccaccio, *Decameron*, p. 12.
16. Boccaccio, *Decameron*, pp. 11–12.
17. Boccaccio, *Decameron*, pp. 12–13.
18. Boccaccio, *Decameron*, pp. 15–16.
19. Jean de Venette, *The Chronicle of Jean de Venette*, trans. Jean Birdsall. New York: Columbia University Press, 1953, pp. 48–49.
20. Quoted in Otto Friedrich, *The End of the World: A History*. New York: Fromm International, 1994, p. 121.
21. Herlihy, *The Black Death and the Transformation of the West*, p. 25.
22. Quoted in Henry Knighton, *The Chronicle of Henry Knighton*, excerpted at: www.mytimemachine.co.uk/blackdeath.htm.
23. Quoted in Friedrich, *The End of the World*, p. 125.

24. Quoted in Barbara W. Tuchman, *A Distant Mirror: The Calamitous 14th Century*. New York: Ballantine, 1996, p. 99.

Chapter Two: Gripped by Fear and Hysteria

25. Venette, *The Chronicle of Jean de Venette*, p. 48.
26. Quoted in Horrox, *The Black Death*, pp. 160–61.
27. Quoted in Horrox, *The Black Death*, pp. 113–14.
28. Tuchman, *A Distant Mirror*, p. 109.
29. "Town of Pistoia: Ordinances for Sanitation in a Time of Mortality," Institute for Advanced Technology in the Humanities, www2.iath.virginia.edu/osheim/pistoia.html.
30. Quoted in Ziegler, *The Black Death*, p. 38.
31. Quoted in Jeffrey Richards, *Sex, Dissidence and Damnation: Minority Groups in the Middle Ages*. New York: Barnes and Noble, 1990, p. 103.
32. James C. Giblin, *When Plague Strikes: The Black Death, Smallpox, AIDS*. New York: HarperCollins, 1997, pp. 32–33.
33. Quoted in Horrox, *The Black Death*, p. 45.
34. Tuchman, *A Distant Mirror*, p. 116.
35. Quoted in Horrox, *The Black Death*, p. 222.
36. Quoted in Horrox, *The Black Death*, p. 208.
37. Quoted in Paul Halsall, ed., "Jewish History Sourcebook: The Black Death and the Jews 1348–1349 C.E.," Internet History Sourcebooks Project, www.fordham.edu/halsall/jewish/1348-jewsblack-death.html

38. Quoted in Halsall, "Jewish History Sourcebook."
39. Quoted in Ziegler, *The Black Death*, p. 67.
40. Quoted in Friedrich, *The End of the World*, p. 126.
41. Quoted in Friedrich, *The End of the World*, p. 126.
42. Quoted in Friedrich, *The End of the World*, p. 129.
43. Friedrich, *The End of the World*, p. 134.

Chapter Three: The Facts About the Plague

44. Herlihy, *The Black Death and the Transformation of the West*, pp. 20–21.
45. Giblin, *When Plague Strikes*, p. 14.
46. Giblin, *When Plague Strikes*, pp. 11–12.
47. Quoted in Nohl, *The Black Death*, p. 20.
48. Bollet, *Plagues and Poxes*, p. 21.
49. Giblin, *When Plague Strikes*, p. 13.
50. Ziegler, *The Black Death*, p. 18.
51. Gottfried, *The Black Death*, p. 4.

Chapter Four: Diverse Economic Effects

52. Quoted in Herlihy, *The Black Death and the Transformation of the West*, p. 41.
53. Gottfried, *The Black Death*, p. 94.
54. Matteo Villani, *Universal Chronicle*, excerpted in Perry M. Rogers, *Aspects of Western Civilization*. Upper Saddler River, NJ: Prentice Hall, 2000, pp. 353–365. Also available at www.u.arizona.edu/~afutrell/w%20civ%2002/plaguereadings.html.
55. Quoted in Herlihy, *The Black Death and the Transformation of the West*, pp. 48–49.

56. Quoted in Friedrich, *The End of the World*, p. 135.
57. Quoted in Rogers, *Aspects of Western Civilization*, p. 365.
58. Herlihy, *The Black Death and the Transformation of the West*, p. 47.
59. Herlihy, *The Black Death and the Transformation of the West*, p. 48.
60. Ziegler, *The Black Death*, p. 199.
61. Quoted in Knighton, *The Chronicle of Henry Knighton*.
62. Quoted in Paul Halsall, ed., "Medieval Source Book: Jean Froissart on the Jacquerie, 1358," Internet History Sourcebooks Project, www.fordham.edu/halsall/source/froissart2.html.
63. Friedrich Lutge, "Germany: The Black Death and a Structural Revolution in Socioeconomic History," in *The Black Death: A Turning Point in History?* ed. William M. Bowsky. New York: Holt, Rinehart and Winston, 1978, p. 84.

Chapter Five: A Host of Cultural Impacts

64. Friedrich, *The End of the World*, pp. 136–37.
65. Venette, *The Chronicle of Jean de Venette*, p. 51.
66. Gottfried, *The Black Death*, p. 89.
67. Johan Huizinga, *The Waning of the Middle Ages*. Mineola, NY: Dover, 1998, p. 134.
68. Tuchman, *A Distant Mirror*, p. 129.
69. Ziegler, *The Black Death*, p. 279.
70. Giblin, *When Plague Strikes*, p. 43.
71. Gottfried, *The Black Death*, p. 142.
72. Gottfried, *The Black Death*, p. 142.
73. Gottfried, *The Black Death*, p. 142.
74. Herlihy, *The Black Death and the Transformation of the West*, pp. 49–50.
75. Quoted in Tuchman, *A Distant Mirror*, p. 124.
76. William H. McNeill, *Plagues and Peoples*, New York: Anchor, 1998, p. 193.

Chapter Six: The Plague in Later Ages

77. Gottfried, *The Black Death*, p. 130.
78. Quoted in John Fenn, *Paston Letters: Original Letters Written During the Reigns of Henry VI, Edward the IV, and Richard III*, vol. 1. London: Charles Knight, 1840, p. 63.
79. Friedrich, *The End of the World*, pp. 137–138.
80. McNeill, *Plagues and Peoples*, p. 23.

Glossary

anti-Semitism: Hatred and prejudice against Jews.

bacteria: A common form of germs.

buboes: Lumps that form under the arms, in the groin, or elsewhere as the result of an infection.

bubonic plague: A deadly disease caused by bacteria, with symptoms including fever, swollen lymph glands, and skin blisters.

cadaver: A dead body.

cleric: A priest or other church official.

contagious: Infectious, or easily passed from one animal or person to another.

ecology: Relating to disease, the manner in which an infection appears and spreads.

epidemiologist: A scientist who studies disease epidemics.

flagellants: People who beat or otherwise mutilate themselves to atone for sins or misdeeds.

indiscriminately: Randomly.

leprosy: A chronic infection that can badly disfigure the face and/or limbs.

lymph nodes: Organs that contain disease-fighting cells and are part of the body's immune system.

macabre: Of a dark or gruesome quality, often pertaining to death.

malnutrition: A serious medical condition caused by the body failing to take in enough nutrients.

manorial system: In medieval Europe, an arrangement in which poor peasants (serfs) lived and worked on a manor (large estate) owned by a wealthy individual.

metaphor: A symbolic comparison of one thing to another.

microbe (or microorganism): A germ or microscopic creature.

omen: A supposedly supernatural sign of an impending event.

optimism: A hopeful, cheerful outlook on life.

ordinance: A decree, law, or public rule.

pessimism: A gloomy, mistrustful outlook on life.

pneumonic plague: A version of plague in which the infection enters the lungs, causing a kind of pneumonia.

reservoir: Relating to disease, a group of animals that carry a disease for an undetermined period of time without passing it to humans.

scapegoat: Someone or something that is falsely blamed for an act or event.

scourge: A whip with spikes attached to its end or ends.

scribe: Mainly in largely illiterate societies, someone who made a living from his or her reading and writing skills.

septicaemic plague: A version of plague in which the infection directly enters the bloodstream, always causing rapid death.

serf: In medieval Europe and elsewhere, a poor worker who was dependent on a wealthy landowner for employment and protection.

symbol: An idea, word, or image that stands for something else.

vector: Relating to disease, a means of transferring an infection from one person or animal to another.

vernacular: The everyday language spoken by a local people.

Yersinia pestis: The bacterium that causes bubonic plague.

For More Information

Books

Giovanni Boccaccio, *Decameron*. Translated by J.G. Nichols. New York: Knopf, 2009. Boccaccio's opening scenes, describing the onset of the Black Death in Florence, still paints a dramatic picture.

Alfred J. Bollet, *Plagues and Poxes: The Impact of Human History on Epidemic Disease*. New York: Demos, 2004. A distinguished medical researcher examines historical disease epidemics, including the outbreak of bubonic plague in the 1300s.

Frederick F. Cartwright and Michael D. Biddiss, *Disease and History*. Stroud, UK: 2004. The authors of this book ably trace the course of major disease epidemics in history.

Otto Friedrich, *The End of the World: A History*. New York: Fromm International, 1994. Extremely well researched and well written, this work singles out key points in history when people thought their world was ending.

James C. Giblin, *When Plague Strikes: The Black Death, Smallpox, AIDS*. New York: HarperCollins, 1997. This is an easy-to-read primer on some classic epidemic diseases.

Robert S. Gottfried, *The Black Death: Natural and Human Disaster in Medieval Europe*. New York: Macmillan, 1985. Filled with useful information, this is one of the best general studies of the Black Death.

John Hatcher, *The Black Death: A Personal History*. New York: Da Capo, 2009. This book re-creates life in an English village during the onslaught of the Black Death.

Rosemary Horrox, ed., *The Black Death*. England: Manchester University Press, 1994. This is a comprehensive collection of primary sources on the Black Death.

John Kelly, *The Great Mortality: An Intimate History of the Black Death*. New York: Harper Perennial, 2006. This is an excellent overview of the onset, devastation, and aftereffects of the Black Death.

Sean Martin, *The Black Death*. Secaucus, NJ: Chartwell, 2009. This book provides a short but fact-filled presentation of the basic facts about the Black Death.

William H. McNeill, *Plagues and Peoples*. New York: Knopf, 1998. One of the great historians of the twentieth century delivers a riveting overview of the role disease has played in history.

Colin Platt, *King Death: The Black Death and Its Aftermath in Late-Medieval England*. Canada: University of Toronto Press, 1997. Platt concentrates on the fairly plentiful eyewitness accounts of the Black Death that have survived in England.

Susan Scott and Christopher Duncan, *Return to the Black Death: The World's Greatest Serial Killer*. New York: Wiley, 2005. The authors discuss the 1300s version of the Black Death as the disease spread from person to person and consider the possibility that it might return in the near future.

Barbara W. Tuchman, *A Distant Mirror: The Calamitous 14th Century*. New York: Ballantine, 1996. This dramatically written volume contains a fulsome chapter describing the demographic, social, and other effects of the Black Death.

Graham Twigg, *The Black Death: A Biological Reappraisal*. New York: Schocken, 1985. This book offers a technical examination of the Black Death, including some alternative theories for what it was.

Philip Ziegler, *The Black Death*. New York: Harper Perennial, 2009. This book offers a comprehensive and thoughtful study by one of the world's leading experts on the subject.

Hans Zinsser, *Rats, Lice and History*. New Brunswick, NJ: Transaction, 2007.

This is a widely popular examination of how tiny bacteria can change the world.

Internet Sources

Paul Halsall, ed., "Jewish History Sourcebook: The Black Death and the Jews 1348–1349 C.E.," Internet History Sourcebooks Project, www.fordham.edu/halsall/jewish/1348-jewsblackdeath.html.

Mike Ibeji, "The Black Death," BBC, November 5, 2009, www.bbc.co.uk/history/british/middle_ages/black_01.shtml.

Websites

Insecta Inspecta World (www.insecta-inspecta.com). This website offers information about insects, including a section about fleas and their role in the spread of the Black Death.

"Plague", MedicineNet.com (www.medicinenet.com/plague/article.htm). Provides an overview of current medical knowledge about bubonic plague and its symptoms and treatment.

Index

class distinction maintenance,
  58–60, *59*
prevalence of pessimist outlook,
  65–67

D
Danse macabre (dance of death),
  66, 66–68
Death, image of, *66,* 66–68
Deaths
  of animals, 24, *25*
  in Avignon, 23
  care of sick and fear of, 8, 15, 21, 23
  disease preparedness and, 14
  in Europe, 8, 38, 76
  during Justinian's Plague, 13
  murder of Jews, 34
  during *pestis secunda,* 77
  during plague cycle, 78
  population increase and, 14–15
  in Venice, 31
  worldwide, 77
Disease reservoirs, 41
Divine punishment as cause, 11, 13, 28

E
Earthquakes, 28, 78
Effects
  charitable giving, 70
  depopulation, 8–9, 38, 71
  economic, 53–58, *55, 56,* 63
  family breakdown, 15, 19
  on learning, 74–75
  medical advances, 74
  moral breakdown, 8, 15, 19, 21–22,
    64–65
  political, *60,* 60–62
  religious, 57, 58, 68–70, *69*
  social, 58–60, *59*
  technological, 71, *72,* 73–74
  See also Labor shortages
Egyptians, ancient, 11
England, 23, 61–62

Epidemiologists, 45
Epizootics, 41
Ergotism, 14
Europe, number of deaths, 8, 38, 76

F
Family, breakdown of, 15, 19
Farming, collapse of manorial system,
  53–56, *55, 56*
Fishing industry, 71
Flagellants, 35–38, *36*
Flagellants' Sermon, 37
Fleas, *42,* 42–43, 48, 80
Florence, Italy, 20
France, *22,* 23, *60,* 62

G
Galen, 50, *50,* 51
Genoese
  Kaffa colony in Crimea, 17–18,
    45, 46
  spread of plague and, 19
Germ theory, 9, 39, 79
Giblin, James C. , 31–32, 42–43, 47,
  69–70
Gottfried, Robert S., 8–9, 49, 56, 65–66,
  71, 77
Greeks, ancient, 12

H
Hansen's disease, 14
Herlihy, David, 24, 39–40, 58, 73–74
Hippocrates, 51
History of plague
  ancient Greeks, 12
  Bible, 9, *10,* 11
  Roman Empire, 12–13
Huizinga, Johan, 67

I
Ibn al-Khatib, 41
Ibn Khatima, 41
Immunity, *49,* 49–50

Impure air hypothesis, 28
Infection theory, 41
Inflation, 58, 60
Italy, 19–22, *29*, 29–31, 70

J
Jacquerie, *60, 62*
Jews, *32, 33,* 33–34, *35*
Justinian's Plague, 12–13

L
Labor shortages
    collapse of manorial system, 53–56,
      55, 56
    construction projects, 70
    technological advances, 71, *72,*
      73–74
    wages and, 56–58, 60, 62
Lake Balkhash, Asia, *16,* 16–17
Languages, 75
Latin, 75
Learning, 74–75
Leprosy, 14
Livestock, care of, 24, *25*
Lower classes, increase in standard of
    living, 56–58
Lymph nodes, 43, *44*

M
Malnutrition, 14
Manorial system, collapse of, 53–56,
    55, 56
Marmots, 17
Measles, 12
Messina, Italy, 19
Meteors, 27
Microbes, 9, 39, 79
Middle Ages and disease, 14
Mongols, 17–18, 46
Moral behavior, breakdown of
    abandonment of sick, 8, 15, 19, 64
    selfishness, 21–22, 65
Movements of planets, 28

O
Old Testament, 11
Omens, 26–28, *27*
Origins, 15–18

P
Palace of the Popes, Avignon, France, *22*
Pasteur, Louis, 79–80, *81*
Peasants
    collapse of manorial system, 53–56,
      55, 56
    rebellions, *60,* 61–62
Pest Maiden, 28–29
Pestis secunda, 77
Petrarch, 67
Physicians, 12, 31, 46, 50–51, 79
Pilgrimages, 70
Pistoia, Italy, *29,* 29–30
Plague cycle, 77–79
Pneumonic plague, 47–48
Political effects, *60,* 60–62
Population
    pre-plague increase, 14–15
    return to pre-plague levels, 8–9, 38
Prayer as treatment, 51
Prevention
    personal immunity, *49,* 49–50
    sanitation, 49
Printing press, *72,* 73–74
Psyche, defined, 64
Pulex irritans, 48

Q
Quarantine measures, 29, 31, 78

R
Rat fleas, *42,* 42–43, 80, 82
Rats, *48*
    black, 41, 43, 46–47, 78
    brown, 78–79
Rebellions
    in England, 61–62
    in France, *60, 62*

Religious effects
  crisis of faith, 68–70, *69*
  increase in fees, 57, 58
Richard II (king of England), 61, 62
Rodents, 17, 41
  See also Rats
Roman Catholic Church, 57, 68–70, *69*
Roman Empire, 12–13
Route of plague, *17,* 18–19
Russia, 23–24

S
Saint Anthony's fire, 14
Sanitation, 49, 79
Scapegoats, 31–33, *32, 33, 35*
Self-flogging, 35–38, *36*
Septicaemic plague, 48–49
Serfs, 53–56, *55*
Siena, Italy, cathedral, 70
Simond, Paul-Louis, 80, 82
Smallpox, 12
Social effects, 58–60, *59*
Sparta, 12
Sumptuary laws, *59,* 60
Symptoms
  classic, 43
  described by eyewitnesses, 9, 20,
    44–45

T
Tartars, 17–18, 46
Technological effects, 71, *72,* 73–74

Thucydides, 12
Trade, *17,* 18–19
Traini, Francesco, 73
Treatment, 50–52
Trinity College, 75
Triumph of Death (Traini), 73
Tuchman, Barbara W., 28–29, 33, 68, 73

U
Universities, 74, 75
University of Prague, 75

V
Vaccines, 79–80
Vectors. *See* Carriers
Venice, Italy, 31

W
Windmills and watermills, 71

X
Xenopsylla cheopis, 42, *42*–43

Y
Yersin, Alexandre, 39–40, 80
Yersinia pestis
  as carriers, 43
  discovered, 39–40, *40*
  forms of disease, 47–49

Z
Ziegler, Philip, 18, 48–49, 60–61, 68

Picture Credits

Cover Photo: © North Wind Picture Archives / Alamy

© AAAC/Topham/The Image Works, 6

© allOver photography/Alamy, 22

© Antiques & Collectables/Alamy, 6

© Bettmann/Corbis, 79

© Biodisc/Visuals Unlimited/Alamy, 42

© Classic Image/Alamy, 15

© Corbis, 16, 51

Courtesy of the Library of Congress, 65, 81

© David Lyons/Alamy, 18

© David Tomlinson/Alamy, 69

© Gianni Dagli Orti/Corbis, 27

© Historical Picture Archive/Corbis, 66

© Hulton-Deutsch Collection/Corbis, 45

© INTERFOTO/Alamy, 7, 10, 49

© Lebrecht Music and Arts Photo Library/ Alamy, 56, 71

© MAPS.com/Corbis, 17

© North Wind Picture Archives / Alamy, 25, 72

© Nucleus Medical Art, Inc./Alamy, 44

© Robert Harding Picture Library Ltd/ Alamy, 29

Roger Viollet Collection/Getty Images, 33

© Sarabjit Singh/Alamy, 35

Science Source/Photo Researchers, Inc, 50, 77

© Scott Camazine/Alamy, 40

Time and Life Pictures/Getty Images, 7

© Terry Whittaker/Alamy, 48

© The Print Collector/Alamy, 32, 36, 55

© TPM Photostock/Alamy, 60

© Vova Pomortzeff/Alamy, 74

© World History Archive/Alamy, 59

About the Author

In addition to his acclaimed volumes on the ancient world, historian Don Nardo has produced several studies of medieval times, including *Life on a Medieval Pilgrimage*, *The Medieval Castle*, *The Vikings*, *The Inquisition*, and a biography of medieval astronomer Tycho Brahe. He has also produced volumes about medieval warfare, the King Arthur legends, and the age of exploration. Mr. Nardo, who also composes orchestral music, resides with his wife, Christine, in Massachusetts.